Business Cards 2
More Ways of Saying Hello

Laurence King Publishing

LAURENCE KING

Published in 2006
by Laurence King Publishing Ltd
71 Great Russell Street
London WC1B 3BP
United Kingdom
Tel_ +44 20 7430 8850
Fax_ +44 20 7430 8880
E_ enquiries@laurenceking.co.uk
www.laurenceking.co.uk

A catalogue record for this book is
available from the British Library.

ISBN-13: 978 1 85669 477 3
ISBN-10: 1 85669 477 1

Printed in China

Words
Liz Farrelly

Design
Michael Dorrian

Selected by
Michael Dorrian
Liz Farrelly

Thank you

Reza Abedini_ Carine Abraham_ Pablo Iglesias Algora_ Tokyo Alice_ Antoine+Manuel_ Jason Arber_ Phil Ashcroft_ David Ashlin_ Paul Ayre_ Jon Barlow_ Scot Bendall_ Sanjai Bhana_ Ric Blackshaw_ Andrew Bowyer_ Mario Buholzer_ Jon Burgerman_ Anthony Burrill_ Rohat Cellali-Sik_ David Choe_ Ricky Churchill_ Jenny Cobden_ Richard Crabb_ Julien Crouigneau_ Mary Crowley_ Mike Curtis_ David Zack Custer_ Constantin Demner_ Miles Donovan_ Emma Dowling_ Gerard Doyle_ Rhonda Drakeford_ Manuel Duboe_ James Lee Duffy_ Neil Edwards_ Brendan Elliot_ Tim Everist_ Troels Faber_ Jim Fenwick_ Lee Ford_ Pete Fowler_ Hugh Frost_ Thorsten Geiger_ Malcolm Goldie_ Joost van der Heijden_ John Hersey_ Antony Hill_ Ella Holliday_ Dave Horwood_ Rian Hughes_ Tony Hung_ Mikhail Iliatov_ Karen Ingram_ Mark James_ Karen Jane_ Tim Jester_ Sarah Kavanagh_ Peter Kellett_ Michaela Kessler_ Ten Kinnei_ Pia Kolle_ Martin Kvamme_ Simon Latarche_ Simone Legno_ Therese Lerfeldt_ Kat Leuzinger_ Harmen Liemburg_ Jo Lightfoot_ David Linderman_ Gavin Lucas_ Joe Lucchese_ Birte Ludwig_ Matthijs Maat_ Cynthia Martinez_ Mimmo Manes_ Rob Manley_ Karl Marin_ Wladimir Marnich_ Mick Marston_ Matthew McCarthy_ John McFaul_ Andrew McGovern_ Scott McGuffie_ Jens Uwe Meyer_ Patrick Miller_ Kate Moross_ Richard Moross_ Dan Moscrop_ Martin Muir_ Martijn Munsters_ Dom Murphy_ Steve Napier_ Jeff Ng_ Richard Niessen_ Jonty O'Connor_ Michael Oliveira-Salac_ Quique Ollervides_ Martijn Oostra_ Nicola Pallett_ Mark Pawson_ Adrian Perry_ Christian Peterson_ Valerie Phillips_ Dan Potter_ Chris Poulton_ Nick Purser_ Reuben Raffael_ Carsten Raffel_ Axel Raidt_ Jasmine Raznahan_ Peter Reddy_ Kate Reik_ David Reinfurt_ Adam Salacuse_ Danny Sangra_ Andy Sargent_ Jenny Scott_ Robert Shore_ Bob Silver_ Jesper Skoog_ Simon Slater_ Kim Smits_ Nick Steel_ Keith Stephenson_ James Sterling_ Jean Jacques Tachdjian_ Kam Tang_ Ben Terrett_ Tofer_ Christiaan Vermaas_ Francesca Wade_ Jonathan Wallace_ Dave Warnke_ Chantal Webber_ Orlando Weeks_ Darren Whittingham_ Klaus Wilhardt_ Jan Wilker_ Will Williams_ Spencer Wilson_ Steve Wilson_ Matt Wingfield_ Ben Wolfinsohn_ Mark Wood_ Woody_ Jen Wu

Special thank you

Ranjit Sehambi_ Gregg Virostek_ Francesca Walton

We're saying "hello" for a second time thanks to the overwhelming response we had to *Business Cards: The Art of Saying Hello* from all the contributors who sent in work (and have sent us more for this book) and from the readers who were pleasantly surprised to find a book about business cards crammed with cutting-edge graphics and unique solutions.

There was nothing run-of-the-mill about that book. We went back to basics and looked for cards that questioned all the conventions, reinvented the wheel and dealt with the changing nature of work and communication. And we found them, in bucketloads.

This time we've cast our net for entries even wider, sending out over two thousand invitations to designers and creative types in every corner of the world. And the payback has been worth the effort, with entries coming in from Buenos Aires, Melbourne, Houston, Liverpool, Tokyo, Copenhagen, Tehran, Dublin, Madrid and Mexico, to name but a few of the more exotic locations.

Instead of finding any obvious cultural differences between cards from east or west, north or south, we've been intrigued by the wide range of creative initiatives, requiring intriguing design solutions, that we've been presented with. From a magazine fetishizing music on vinyl to online game-playing clubs, from an agency for all manner of young creatives, run by young creatives, to a shop that sells pebbles and a guerrilla-marketing company that employs the most uncompromising street-inspired artists.

One of the themes running through this collection is flexibility. Fuelled by the fact that you can inkjet-print a different card every day, or tack a couple of designs onto a litho print run, designers are taking the opportunity to produce frequently changing series of cards, tailoring them to different needs and clients, or making a selection simply depending on how they feel that day. Illustrators take it even further, creating handmade cards for special friends. Adding a provocative message means you can tell the person you're handing a card to not just something about yourself, but also what you think of them. This tactic may get you into trouble, so be nice!

With so many ways of communicating these days, and the fact that some creative types really do have nomadic lifestyles, the alternative to loading a card with contact details – from email to snail mail, plus two or three different mobile numbers and various websites representing any number of businesses – is to say nothing at all. Cards presenting an enigmatic personality, or more than one, hinting at the holder's multiple talents, need show no more than a name, or even simply a blank space, and afford infinite opportunity for customization.

Holding someone's card in your hand creates a very special type of contact, so why not think about how that experience could play out? A box of goodies that requires your invited participants to sit, sift and be amazed by the contents of that box and by extension of your brain; paper cards hand-stitched with multi-coloured thread that cause them to marvel at the patience required; wooden cards branded with hot-metal that might suggest you like to play with fire; a game of cards, to be arranged and rearranged and which can reveal any number of meanings. You'll find just such solutions here. Remember, though, there is no one way, no right way and no wrong way; whatever you want to say, just say it, whatever way you choose... that's the art of the business card.

If you would like to contribute to a third book in this series, please send your cards to the publisher's office, marked for our attention. There they will live in a large box until we get around to it, in about a year or so... and don't forget to tell us something about yourself and why you chose to make your card the way you did.

But if you fuck with us we'll cut your fucking nuts off Florence

florencefineart.com

Design
Saturday

For
Florence_
Agency/gallery_
London, UK

Info
A cool and sophisticated identity for a contemporary gallery run
by female directors utilizes ice-blue print and silver-foil blocking.
There are two versions of the business card; while one is polite,
the other delivers a withering one-liner and is offered to friends
with a sense of humour.

Yes we are ladies who love pretty things

But if you fuck with us we'll cut your fucking nuts off Florence florencefineart.com

Florence
10 Stephen Mews
London W1T 1AG

www.
florencefineart.
com

Telephone
+44
(0)207307
3145

hey wake up

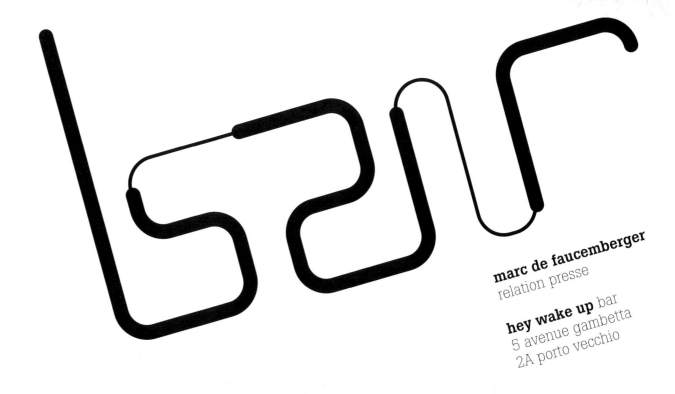

marc de faucemberger
relation presse

hey wake up bar
5 avenue gambetta
2A porto vecchio

<u>Design</u>
June

<u>For</u>
Hey Wake Up_
Bar_
Porto Vecchio, Italy

<u>Info</u>
An elegant abstraction of a neon sign announces this trend-
setting bar. It delivers a strong message via a dynamic
logotype, and it's only when you turn the card over that you
realize it's for a bar. Don't take it personally!

Jenny Cobden

T: +44(0)7810580990
W: www.posikids.org

Jenny Cobden

T: +44(0)7810580990
W: www.posikids.org

Jenny Cobden

T: +44(0)7810580990
W: www.posikids.org

Jenny Cobden

T: +44(0)7810580990
W: www.posikids.org

Jenny Cobden

T: +44(0)7810580990
W: www.posikids.org

Design
Jenny Cobden

For
Jenny Cobden_
Designer_
Brighton, UK

Info
Jenny Cobden's set of ten cards fit together
to spell out a big bold "hello".

Jenny Cobden

T: +44(0)7810580990
W: www.posikids.org

Jenny Cobden

T: +44(0)7810580990
W: www.posikids.org

Jenny Cobden

T: +44(0)7810580990
W: www.posikids.org

Jenny Cobden

T: +44(0)7810580990
W: www.posikids.org

Jenny Cobden

T: +44(0)7810580990
W: www.posikids.org

Hi, my name is Lee and I'm a Senior Designer at Fold7.

When I was age 7, I wanted to drive a talking black car with a flashing red light at the front.

Fold7

Hi, my name is Harvey and I'm a Senior Artworker/Designer at Fold7.

When I was age 7, I wanted to be a Ye Olde English Pub Landlord.

Fold7

Hi, my name is Letizia and I'm a Project Manager at Fold7.

When I was age 7, I was told I was destined to be a frisbee champion.

Fold7

Hi, my name is Tony and I'm an Accountant at Fold7.

When I was age 7, I wanted be flying down the wing like John Barnes.

Fold7

Hi, my name is Nikki and I'm a Creative Director at Fold7.

When I was age 7, I wanted to be David Soul's girlfriend.

Fold7

Hi, my name is Charlie and I'm a Senior Designer at Fold7.

When I was age 7, I wanted to be an intergalactic smuggler just like Han Solo.

Fold7

Hi, my name is Natalie and I'm a Producer at Fold7.

When I was age 7, I wanted to marry Marti Pellow from Wet Wet Wet.

I was their biggest fan!

Fold7

Hi, my name is Joe and I'm a Designer at Fold7.

When I was age 7, I wanted to be He-Man, Master of the Universe.

Fold7

Design
Fold 7

For
Fold 7_
Designers_
London, UK

Info
An understated typographic solution for a design studio, home to many different personalities, this series of cards supplies the answer to one of life's most poignant questions: "What did you want to be when you were seven?"

Hi, my name is Chimp and I'm in charge of Special Projects at Fold7.

When I was age 7, I wanted to be your Knight in shining armour.

Fold7

Hi, my name is Kelly and I'm a Studio Manager/Assistant Producer at Fold7.

When I was age 7, I wanted to be Cheetara, the fastest of the Thundercats!

Fold7

Hi, my name is John and I'm a Motion Graphics Designer at Fold7.

When I was 7, I wanted to solve mysteries with the Red Hand Gang.

Fold7

Hi, my name is Claire and I'm a Project Manager at Fold7.

When I was age 7, I wanted to be a butterfly.

Fold7

Hi, my name is Chris and I'm a Senior Designer at Fold7.

When I was age 7, I wanted to be Jive Talkin' and Down In The Tube Station At Midnight.

Fold7

Hi, my name is Nic and I'm a Motion Graphics Designer at Fold7.

When I was age 7, I wanted to be much older, like eight.

Fold7

Hi, my name is John and I'm a Senior Art Director at Fold7.

When I was age 7, I wanted to be an adult.

Fold7

Hi, we are Fold7, a creative led, cross media communications agency.

We work extensively in Design, Web, Advertising, Marketing, Brand Strategy and Brand Building.

Fold7

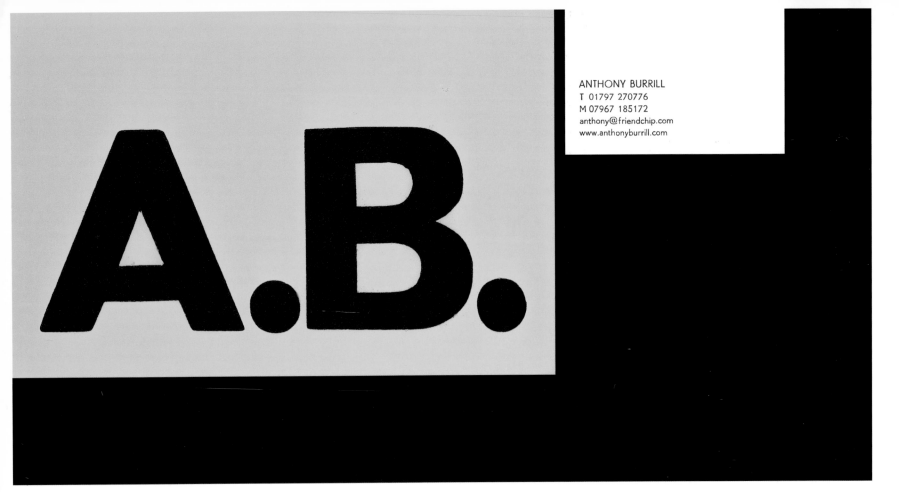

ANTHONY BURRILL
T 01797 270776
M 07967 185172
anthony@friendchip.com
www.anthonyburrill.com

Design
  Anthony Burrill

For
  Anthony Burrill_
  Designer_
  London, UK

Info
  A veteran of self-publishing, well known for his books and
  limited-edition posters, Anthony Burrill brings the bold aesthetic
  of wood-block type to his business card; and how appropriate
  that the initials of an aficionado of type should start the alphabet.

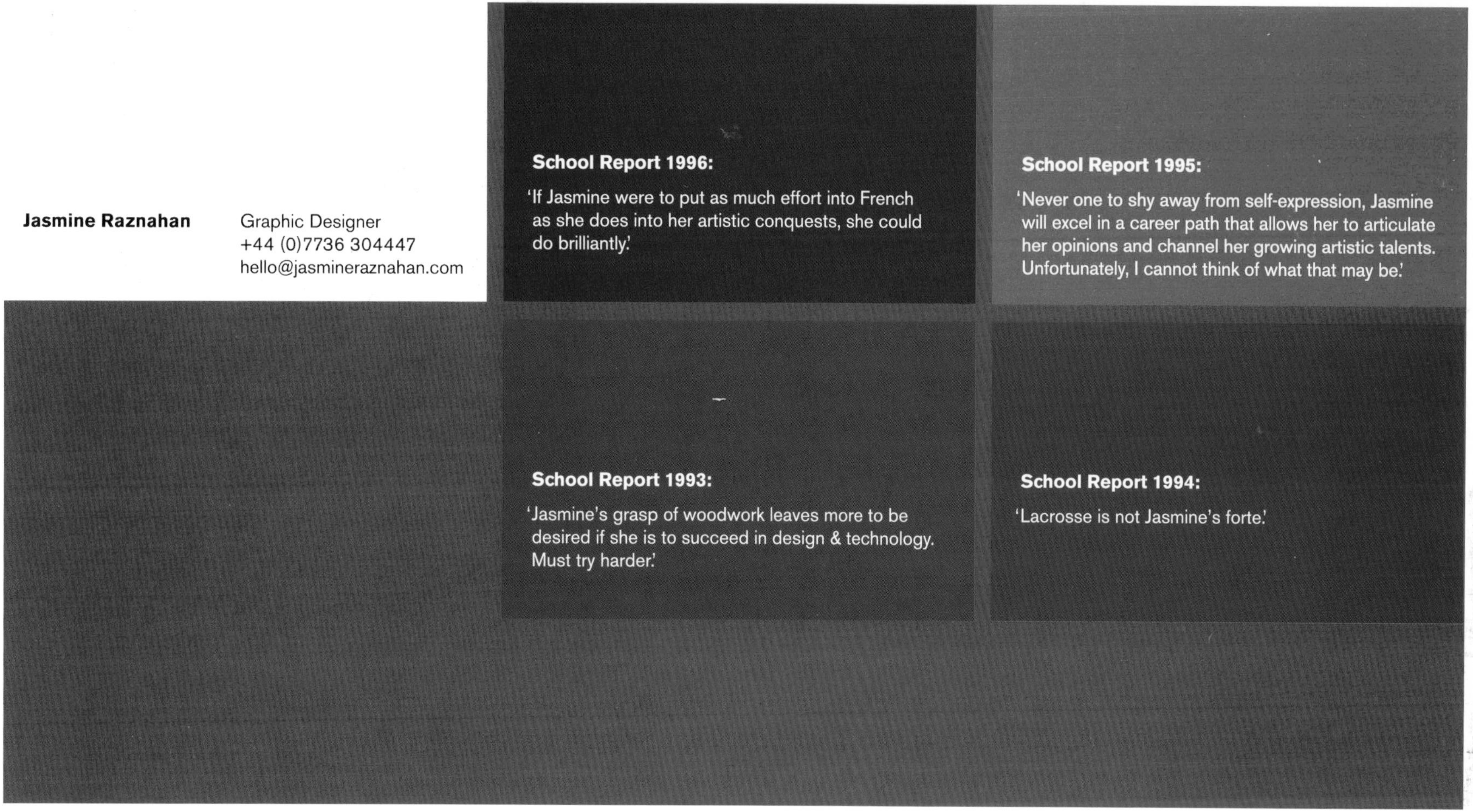

Jasmine Raznahan

Graphic Designer
+44 (0)7736 304447
hello@jasmineraznahan.com

School Report 1996:

'If Jasmine were to put as much effort into French as she does into her artistic conquests, she could do brilliantly.'

School Report 1995:

'Never one to shy away from self-expression, Jasmine will excel in a career path that allows her to articulate her opinions and channel her growing artistic talents. Unfortunately, I cannot think of what that may be.'

School Report 1993:

'Jasmine's grasp of woodwork leaves more to be desired if she is to succeed in design & technology. Must try harder.'

School Report 1994:

'Lacrosse is not Jasmine's forte.'

Design
Jasmine Raznahan

For
Jasmine Raznahan_
Designer_
London, UK

Info
Echoing her cerebral approach to design, which is also deceptively entertaining, Jasmine Raznahan's set of cards (in shades of school uniforms) presents humorous snippets from teachers' reports. Reading between the lines, she's chosen just the right career path.

Ewan MacLeod

11 Golden Square, London, W1F 9JB.
T: +44 (0)20 7300 3555. F: +44 (0)20 7494 3288.
E: ewanm@goldensq.com www.goldensq.com

EXT. WELSH SEASIDE, BEACH SETTING – DAY

FIONA V/O
"What the f*!k was that?"

SHARON V/O
"I dunno, but it looks pretty."
(in a vacant tone)

Meanwhile we have witnessed three alien mechanoids floating through the dispersing vapour cloud and heading towards the two bronzed beauties on the sub-tropical beach.

We follow a man who is being buffeted by gale-force winds as he struggles to walk down a busy road. At the same time endeavouring to tell us about the benefits of life-insurance.

The wind now turns to driving rain, then marble-sized hailstones; a grand piano smashes down onto the pavement beside him, followed by bolts of lightning that narrowly miss him.

SFX: The sound of wind, driving rain, thunder and lightning.

The camera pulls out to reveal that he is the only pedestrian being affected by these bizarre acts of God, while those around him casually go about their business.

TONY V/O: "Second left after the phone and the coffee cup."

SARAH V/O: "Left after the coffee cup, right."

Cut to a tracking shot along a kitchen work-surface, past the phone and around the kettle. We now see Sarah scale the gigantic pack of breakfast cereal and climb inside.

SARAH V/O: Muffled munching sounds coming from within the cereal packet.

The packet starts to bulge and splits at the seams and we see Sarah rapidly grow from 3 inches to 5 foot 7 inches, and sitting on the kitchen work-surface.

SFX: MUSIC UP. (Imagine by J. Lennon)
We open on a head and shoulders shot of Fidel Castro singing the lyrics to camera.

As we watch, we see the worlds leaders seamlessly morph into each other, all the time singing "Imagine".

Fidel Castro into Ronald Reagan into Gorbachev into Kofi Annan into Saddam Hussein into George W Bush into Tony Blair and so on.

We open on a scenic shot of the Serengeti with antelope, zebra and buffalo milling about.

(We hear a country and western tune strike up.)

Cut to a c/u of a zebra talking to an antelope.

VO: Zebra: Oh I love this one, it's one of my favourites!

Cut back to the antelope singing along to Dolly Parton.

VO: Antelope: Working 9-5, what a way to make a living.

Cutting to a wide shot, we see the hordes of zebra, antelope and buffalo line dancing in time to the music and singing along.

The camera tracks continuously alongside the singer as he walks to the corner shop, oblivious to the mayhem he is causing.

We follow him as he casually walks across a dual-carriageway, narrowly missing trucks and cars as they swerve to avoid him. Setting off an escalating chain of events, he is turning the sleepy town of Swindon into a place that resembles an apocalyptic nightmare.

V/O: SINGER: Just a pint of milk, cheers.

We open above the clouds; the camera descends into the heart of the metropolis, a city gone mad, overcrowded, automated and claustrophobic.

We track along vast bustling city streets, over the roofs of stationary traffic, bumper to bumper.

The camera stops at one car window. A man sitting behind the steering wheel smiles to himself. The camera tracks through the window into the car, we now find ourselves on a deserted beach with the sound of crashing waves and the same man still smiling lying on a sun lounger.

We open on **two bacteria in a Petri dish having a conversation about the meaning of life.**

V/O: BACTERIA 1, "There's got to be more to life than continually sub-dividing and multiplying, aint there?"

Cut to a wide shot of a technician in a white lab coat sitting down to look through a microscope. **Cut to the technicians p.o.v. down the microscope.**

V/O: BACTERIA 2, "Yes I have this underlying feeling that we are part of some big master plan and just a mere piece of this jigsaw puzzle we call life."

A deliveryman enters with a box containing 50 tortoises to promote the new and improved long-lasting, hardwearing paint.

VO: Store person 1: Not more of those **talking tortoises** to give away, we still have a load in the warehouse, back-chatting the staff.

Cut to ten of the tortoises on the counter, precariously balanced in a tortoise pyramid.

VO: Deliveryman: "Sign 'ere mate."

Cut back to the 50 tortoises singing "This old house" in unison and swaying back and forth.

We follow the day in the life of a topsy-turvy world. **Where the sky is green, the grass is blue, ducks clinch business deals on mobile phones and humans bark, chase sticks and run around on all fours.**

Cut to a business meeting in a restaurant, between two mallards, a drake and a coot.

V/O: DUCK 1: **"Bill please!"**

Cut to a huge metal demolition ball as it swings in slow motion from a crane. **We follow the ball,** cutting quickly between it and an unsuspecting greenhouse.

In extreme slow motion we see the demolition ball impact the greenhouse. The greenhouse stands resolute and unscathed, but the wrecking ball cracks, then shatters into a thousand tiny pieces.

Cut to a wide shot, **we see the whole crane shatter as if made of porcelain.**

We open on a **six-month-old baby sat in an armchair, talking directly to camera, he tells us how it used to be in the good old days.**

V/O: I remember when Curly Wurlys were 5p, and all these were still fields, when Britain was not dictated to by Brussels and when a figurehead wasn't just for stamps.

He continues his diatribe at length, becoming more and more **enraged and gesticulating wildly,** until he bursts into floods of tears.

He is **falling through the air hurtling towards the ground.** We watch him closely as he calmly pulls a prawn sandwich from his huge beard as he falls. After eating it, **he pulls out a wheel hub and car tyre** followed by a kitchen sink, eventually **pulling out an umbrella.**

He **opens it and gently glides down to earth (Mary Poppins style),** and then walks off scratching his bum.

Cut to the blood-red F1 car, flicking through the chicane **at warp speed as if it were on rails. The F1 car** seamlessly morphes into a hand-held razor, gliding smoothly over the contours of a well defined jaw line.

We now **zoom into the razor blades, to see individual hairs being felled like tree trunks** in incredible close up.

We open on a small boy walking down the road. He breaks into a jog (the camera tracking alongside him).

As he runs faster and faster, the boy **gradually turns into a young man, then a full-grown adult; clothes rip, shoes tear, the leaves fall from the trees and snow starts to fall.**

The boy suddenly stops running **and he is now an old man with white hair and a long grey beard.**

VO: This offer is for life; it doesn't run out until you do.

The old man looks to camera and smiles, then sets off running again.

Design
Julian Harriman-
Dickinson_
Nick Steel

Copywriting
Julian Harriman-
Dickinson

For
Golden Square_
Post-production_
London, UK

Info
Created for a post-production company specializing in FX, each card in the series presents a script tailored to a staff member; sequences of special effects are highlighted with fluorescent ink.

Bo Lundberg Illustration AB
Sten Bergmans väg 25
SE-121 46 Johanneshov
Telephone: +46 8 643 5054
Fax: +46 8 643 8950
Mobile: +46 70 327 6734
E-mail: bo@bolundberg.com
Web: www.bolundberg.com

Bo Lundberg Illustration AB
Sten Bergmans väg 25
SE-121 46 Johanneshov
Telephone: +46 8 643 5054
Fax: +46 8 643 8950
Mobile: +46 70 327 6734
E-mail: bo@bolundberg.com
Web: www.bolundberg.com

Bo Lundberg Illustration AB
Sten Bergmans väg 25
SE-121 46 Johanneshov
Telephone: +46 8 643 5054
Fax: +46 8 643 8950
Mobile: +46 70 327 6734
E-mail: bo@bolundberg.com
Web: www.bolundberg.com

Bo Lundberg Illustration AB
Sten Bergmans väg 25
SE-121 46 Johanneshov
Telephone: +46 8 643 5054
Fax: +46 8 643 8950
Mobile: +46 70 327 6734
E-mail: bo@bolundberg.com
Web: www.bolundberg.com

Design
 Marnich Design

For
 Bo Lundberg_
 Illustrator_
 Johanneshov,
 Sweden

Info
 Cool, sophisticated, direct – an illustrator's first name becomes
 an abstracted logo realized in a series of eye-catching colours.

James Joyce
james@itsbiggerthan.com
www.itsbiggerthan.com
07812 456 247

Maxim Cockett
maxim@itsbiggerthan.com
www.itsbiggerthan.com
07837 524 061

Leo Walton
leo@itsbiggerthan.com
www.itsbiggerthan.com
07718 254 097

Gavin Lucas
gavin@itsbiggerthan.com
www.itsbiggerthan.com
07907 449 691

Sam Willis
sam@itsbiggerthan.com
www.itsbiggerthan.com
07818 068 996

Design
One Fine Day

For
It's Bigger Than_
Club promoters_
London, UK

Info
Created for club promoters who set out to replicate the best
house party you'll ever experience, putting the audience centre
stage via an eclectic play list that makes everyone feel at home,
these colour-coded cards simply shout about what they do.

NATALIE HENKEL
birdstar entertainment ohg

Vogelsmühle 13–17
D-42477 Radevormwald
fon +49 (0) 21 91- 4 69 36 72
fax +49 (0) 21 91- 96 31 89
mobil +49 (0) 172- 6 39 46 25
henkel@birdstar.de · www.birdstar.de

Design
Pia Kolle

For
Birdstar
Entertainment_
Production company_
Cologne, Germany

Info
The company logotype is split and printed front and back,
maximizing point size and emphasizing the name's two elements.

Design
Unit Delta Plus

For
Sebastian Ludvigsen_
Photographer_
Oslo, Norway

Info
Created for a photographer who specializes in glamorous fashion
and music shoots, this card, complete with stars, hearts, bubbles
and silver-foil targets, is a perfect fit.

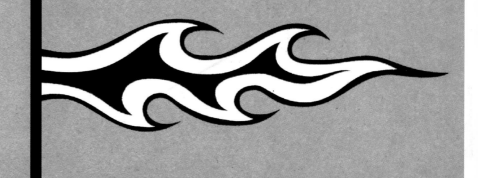

karlssonwilker inc.

536 6th avenue
2nd and 3rd floor
new york, ny 10011

jan wilker

t 001 212 929 8064
f 001 212 929 8063
tellmewhy@karlssonwilker.com

Design
Karlsson Wilker Inc

For
Karlsson Wilker Inc_
Designers_
New York, USA

Info
This suitably jet-powered logo is for a design company with a bold, edgy aesthetic, specializing in music packaging. The flame (in uncharacteristic black and white), teamed with blocks of information and printed on grey board, is both tactile and iconic.

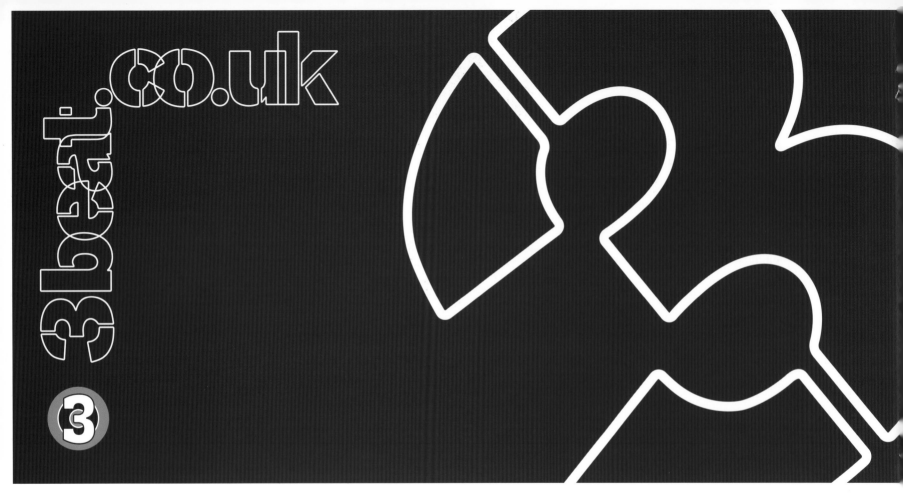

Design
Plast■c
Gerard Doyle

For
3 Beat Records_
Record label_
Liverpool, UK

Info
On this card for one of the UK's most successful dance-music retailers, a distinctive outline logo is abstracted to maximum effect.

3beatrecords

pezz.

5 Slater Street, Liverpool, L1 4BW
telephone +44[0]151 709 3355
mobile +44[0]7976 800 022
email pezz@3beat.co.uk

3beat.co.uk

CHAMBERMADE

DOUGLAS HORTON
ARTISTIC DIRECTOR

PHONE +61 3 9329 7422
FAX +61 3 9329 7434
DOUGLAS@CHAMBERMADE.ORG.AU
CHAMBERMADE.ORG.AU

ARTS HOUSE
NORTH MELBOURNE TOWNHALL
CNR QUEENSBERRY & ERROL STREET
PO BOX 302 NORTH MELBOURNE
VICTORIA 3051 AUSTRALIA

ROBINA BURTON
GENERAL MANAGER

PHONE +61 3 9329 7422
FAX +61 3 9329 7434
ROBINA@CHAMBERMADE.ORG.AU
CHAMBERMADE.ORG.AU

ARTS HOUSE
NORTH MELBOURNE TOWNHALL
CNR QUEENSBERRY & ERROL STREET
PO BOX 302 NORTH MELBOURNE
VICTORIA 3051 AUSTRALIA

Design
Clear

For
Chamber Made_
Music-theatre
production_
Melbourne,
Australia

Info
Subtle variations of a two-colour, line-and-dot motif are used
to delineate between staffers at Chamber Made, Australia's
independent production company for contemporary music
theatre.

IRENE GUZOWSKI
MARKETING COORDINATOR

PHONE +61 3 9329 7422
FAX +61 3 9329 7434
IRENE@CHAMBERMADE.ORG.AU
CHAMBERMADE.ORG.AU

ARTS HOUSE
NORTH MELBOURNE TOWNHALL
CNR QUEENSBERRY & ERROL STREET
PO BOX 302 NORTH MELBOURNE
VICTORIA 3051 AUSTRALIA

JACINTA KENNEDY
ADMINISTRATOR

PHONE +61 3 9329 7422
FAX +61 3 9329 7434
JACINTA@CHAMBERMADE.ORG.AU
CHAMBERMADE.ORG.AU

ARTS HOUSE
NORTH MELBOURNE TOWNHALL
CNR QUEENSBERRY & ERROL STREET
PO BOX 302 NORTH MELBOURNE
VICTORIA 3051 AUSTRALIA

ROBINA BURTON
GENERAL MANAGER

PHONE +61 3 9329 7422
FAX +61 3 9329 7434
ROBINA@CHAMBERMADE.ORG.AU
CHAMBERMADE.ORG.AU

ARTS HOUSE
NORTH MELBOURNE TOWNHALL
CNR QUEENSBERRY & ERROL STREET
PO BOX 302 NORTH MELBOURNE
VICTORIA 3051 AUSTRALIA

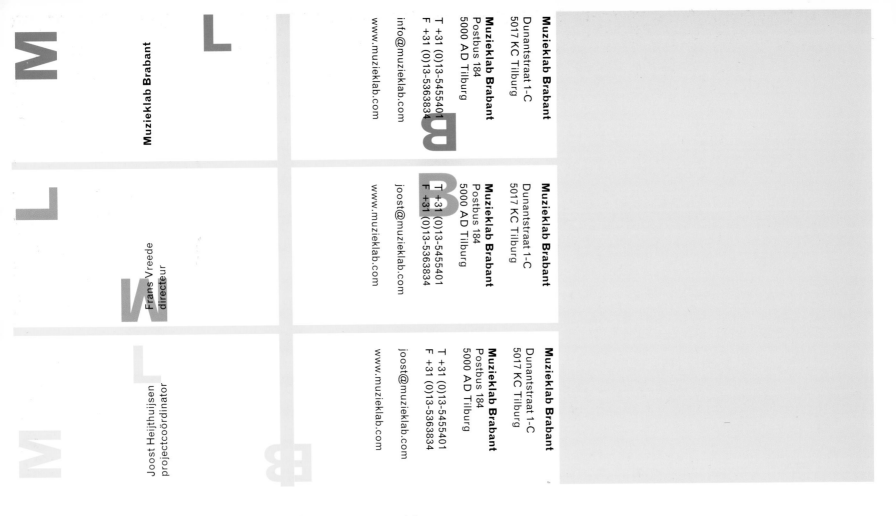

Muzieklab Brabant

Muzieklab Brabant
Dunantstraat 1-C
5017 KC Tilburg

Muzieklab Brabant
Postbus 184
5000 AD Tilburg

T +31 (0)13-5455401
F +31 (0)13-5363834

info@muzieklab.com

www.muzieklab.com

Muzieklab Brabant
Dunantstraat 1-C
5017 KC Tilburg

Muzieklab Brabant
Postbus 184
5000 AD Tilburg

T +31 (0)13-5455401
F +31 (0)13-5363834

joost@muzieklab.com

www.muzieklab.com

Muzieklab Brabant
Dunantstraat 1-C
5017 KC Tilburg

Muzieklab Brabant
Postbus 184
5000 AD Tilburg

T +31 (0)13-5455401
F +31 (0)13-5363834

joost@muzieklab.com

www.muzieklab.com

Frans Vreede
directeur

Joost Heijthuijsen
projectcoördinator

<u>Design</u>
Mikhail Iliatov

<u>For</u>
Muzieklab Brabant_
Music producer_
Tilburg,
The Netherlands

<u>Info</u>
Mikhail Iliatov designed a stationery grid based on 12 notes
on a stave for a Dutch music producer; the letters M, L and B are
positioned on the grid in the shape of various musical chords.

Design
Niche

For
Hands On_
Holistic body work_
London, UK

Info
A folding card provides space to write appointment times for
this holistic therapist, while a rainbow-esque logo hints at light
and energy.

DANIEL SCHWEIZER
1, VILLA DE SÉGUR 75007 PARIS
TÉL: +33 (0) 143 70 53 83 FAX: +33 (0) 143 7
MOB: +33 (0) 608 27 75 25
E-MAIL: CONTACT@DANIEL-SCHWEIZER.
AGENT: CONTACT@CLARISSECANTELO

Design
Antoine+Manuel

For
Daniel Schweizer_
Photographer_
Paris, France

Info
Glitzy foil-blocking reflects the glamorous nature of this still-life
and beauty photographer's work, while the abstract icon hints
at the painstaking technical requirements of creating such
pristine images.

Clusta LTD

MATTHEW CLUGSTON

STUDIO 103 / 104 THE CUSTARD FACTORY
GIBB STREET BIRMINGHAM UK B9 4AA

T: +44 (0) 121 604 0004
F: +44 (0) 121 604 3344
M: +44 (0) 7970 208 554
E: matt@clusta.com
www.clusta.com

Clusta LTD

Design
Clusta

For
Clusta_
Designers_
Birmingham, UK

Info
An abstract orange icon punctuates a subtle all-over grey-on-white pattern; this design company, specializing in digitally delivered solutions, seamlessly marries image-making and technology.

Torgeir Gullaksen
Promoter

Phone: +47 22 33 70 99
Fax: +47 22 42 87 88
Mobile: +47 91 63 67 47
torgeir@goldstar.no

Goldstar Music AS
Grensen 9
N-0159 Oslo
Norway

www.goldstar.no

<u>Design</u>
Unit Delta Plus

<u>For</u>
Goldstar Music_
Music management_
Oslo, Norway

<u>Info</u>
An eye-catching logo in gold and red, reminiscent of a
once-powerful empire, is paired with suitably baroque type.

PUNKROK RECORDS
E: INFO@PUNKROK.COM
WWW.PUNKROK.COM

Design
Clusta

For
Punkrok Records_
DJ/producer_
Birmingham, UK

Info
The mixed genres of black letter-style type and finely drawn silhouetted foliage echo the dual incarnation of James Algate, a DJ who also produces.

Design
ArthurSteenHorne
Adamson

For
Drugstore_
Talent agency_
London, UK

Info
A unique recruitment agency that assembles teams of creative
freelancers on a project-by-project basis is branded along the
lines of a turn-of-the-century American drugstore, combining an
Art Nouveau floral motif, traditional typeface and a pick'n'mix
colour scheme.

CENTRE NATIONAL
DE DANSE CONTEMPORAINE
ANGERS

CNDC.FR

CENTRE NATIONAL
DE DANSE CONTEMPORAINE
ANGERS

Christophe Susset
secrétaire général
christophe.susset@cndc.fr

CNDC \ 42, BD HENRI-ARNAULD \ BP 50107 \ 49101 ANGERS CEDEX 02
TÉL. +33 (0)241 24 12 12 \ FAX +33 (0)241 24 12 00
DIRECTION ARTISTIQUE EMMANUELLE HUYNH

Design
Antoine+Manuel

For
CNDC_
Dance centre_
Angers, France

Info
Organic, quirky and die-cut, featuring the designers' signature
sinuous drawing, the identity and card for France's national
centre and school for contemporary dance reflect the dynamic,
unpredictable and boundary-breaking nature of the creativity
nurtured there.

fairlife

Shun Ran

web
http://www.fairlife.jp

mail
kazunokokazunoko@hotmail.com

fair life
studio

web
http://www.fairlife.jp

7-12-5-105
hunabashi, setagaya-ku
Tokyo - JAPAN
156-0055

Kimio Mizutani
e-mail : fairlife@mac.com
mobile : (81) 090 2933 3510

phone
(81) 03-5490-1551
fax
(81) 03-4400-5028

Design
  Carine Abraham

For
  Fairlife_
  Sound studio_
  Tokyo, Japan

Info
  Organic leaf, wave and cloud forms, suggesting traditional
  Japanese wood-block designs, are assembled together into
  various combinations.

fair life
studio

Kimio Mizutani

mobile :
(81) 090 2933 3510

web :
http://www.fairlife.jp

fairlife

Sakurai Takamasa

mail
sakusaku@dhw.co.jp

web
http://www.fairlife.jp

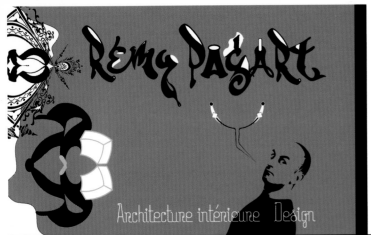

Rémy Pagart

Architecture intérieure Design

2 rue Pasteur
59 890
Quesnoy sur Deule

Tel-fax:
03.20.78.69.68
06.85.84.50.99

tragga@wanadoo.fr

2 rue Pasteur
59 890
Quesnoy sur Deule

Tel-fax:
03.20.78.69.68
06.85.84.50.99

tragga@wanadoo.fr

Ymer Tragga

sculptures

Design
 Jean Jacques
 Tachdjian

For
 Rémy Pagart_
 Designer/sculptor_
 Quesnoy sur Deule,
 France

Info
 Subtle variations on a theme, using intricate patterns and type
 repeated at various scales, differentiate a series of cards for this
 creative individual's multiple job titles.

Ric Blackshaw
Creative Director
ric@scrawlcollective.co.uk

Scrawl Collective
Illustration & Design agen cy
3-4 Bartholomew Place
London EC1A 7HH

T +44 (0) 20 7600 4700
M +44 (0) 7770 888 104

www.scrawlcollective.co.uk

Ric Blackshaw
Creative Director
ric@scrawlcollective.co.uk

Scrawl Collective
Illustration & Design agen cy
3-4 Bartholomew Place
London EC1A 7HH

T +44 (0) 20 7600 4700
M +44 (0) 7770 888 104

www.scrawlcollective.co.uk

Ric Blackshaw
Creative Director
ric@scrawlcollective.co.uk

Scrawl Collective
Illustration & Design agen cy
3-4 Bartholomew Place
London EC1A 7HH

T +44 (0) 20 7600 4700
M +44 (0) 7770 888 104

www.scrawlcollective.co.uk

Design
Ric Blackshaw_
Niche_
Tim Shandro

Illustration
Phlash

For
Scrawl Collective_
Art agency_
London, UK

Info
Featuring Phlash's unmistakable creature alongside detailed,
baroque lettering, these cards hint at the mix of aesthetics
offered by this creative agency.

Bliss

Geraldine Soussan

DELHIR INC DBAs BLISS

gsoussan@hotmail.com

169 Manhattan Avenue suite 6E · New York, New York 10025 USA
Tel. (1) 212 678 08 50

Rehov Hamagid # 19 Jerusalem, 93114 ISRAEL
Tel. (972) 2 563 01 62

<u>Design</u>
Jean Jacques
Tachdjian

<u>For</u>
Bliss_
Textile designers_
New York, USA
Jerusalem, Israel

<u>Info</u>
This textile designer's card hints at a love of surface
pattern, combining baroque elements in a playful and
contemporary style.

Design
Multistorey

For
Whoopee_
Artists' agency_
London, UK

Info
This artists' agency specializes in burlesque acts and is run by fans of vintage ephemera. Aiming to capture the quality of Victorian-era printing, the card's dimensions are based on traditional paper sizes: a pale-peach stock is delicately embossed, the logo is foil-blocked and debossed in old gold, and the card's edges are deckled and goldleafed.

Design
Rob Manley_
Pete Fowler

For
Playbeast_
Designers/
manufacturers_
London, UK

Info
The distribution arm of Pete Fowler's Monsterism empire,
Playbeast features a suitably ambiguous aesthetic, denoting
that these toys are for big boys.

Design
 David Zack Custer

For
 HandGun_
 Designer_
 Portland, USA

Info
 Deliberately provocative, the HandGun aesthetic of mock-
military, techno-retro is realized on this card via a combination
of wood grain, info boxes and faux-Japanese lettering.

John McFaul
+44 (0)7740 704 989
studio@mcfaul.net

www.mcfaul.net

Design
  John McFaul

For
  McFaul_
  Designer_
  Chichester, UK

Info
  A message for every occasion: McFaul uses UV varnish to subtly
reinforce a number of one-liners he's likely to use on new clients.
These business cards double as swing-tags for his online clothing
label.

UNITED GAMING FORCES

WWW.UGF-CLAN.COM

Design
Chemicalbox

For
United Gaming
Forces_
Network Game Team_
Biel, Switzerland

Info
No-nonsense black and white typography, teamed with a forbidding coat of arms, adds gravitas to this online game-playing community.

PRE-

PRE-BRANDING
BOX 11207, 100 61 STOCKHOLM
NORRLANDSGATAN 31
TEL +46 8 644 99 55
FAX +46 70 383 50 07
INFO@PRE-BRANDING.SE
WWW.PRE-BRANDING.SE

<u>Design</u>
Gabor Palotai
Design

<u>For</u>
Pre-Branding_
Consultant_
Stockholm, Sweden

<u>Info</u>
Referencing the black and white pixellated style of early digital
displays, Gabor Palotai goes back to basics for a company
that improves communication between agencies, clients and
the public.

Design
Ten Kinnei

For
TenTenTen_
Designer_
Tokyo, Japan

Info
A square card, an illustration and type based on pixels,
albeit more playful than scientific, highlight this designer's
numeric name.

Design
Zookeeper

For
Zookeeper_
Designer_
France

Info
 Custom type, a "kanji"-style logo and die-cut form imbue
 this card with the streety excitement of a club flyer.

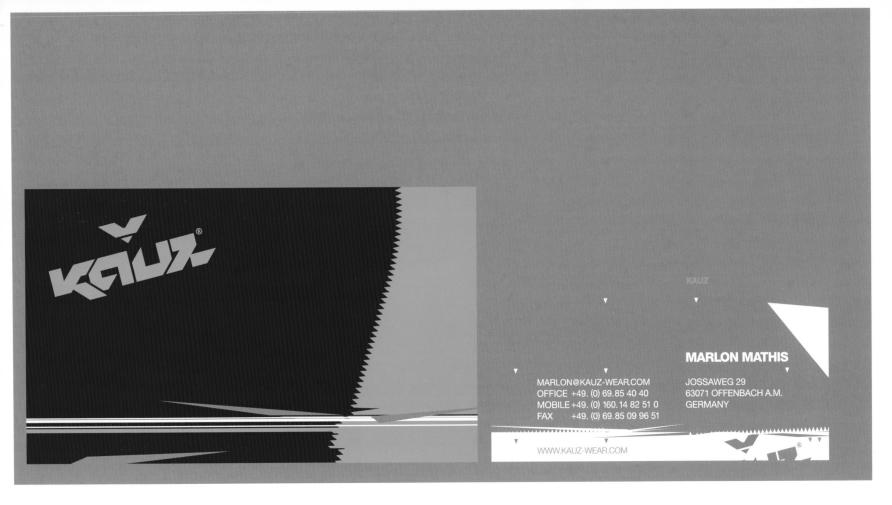

Design
  Viagrafik

For_
  Kauz_
  Clothing label_
  Offenbach,
  Germany

Info
  A streetwear label is treated to a dynamic, high-contrast
  aesthetic, reminiscent of pattern markings and cutting tools.

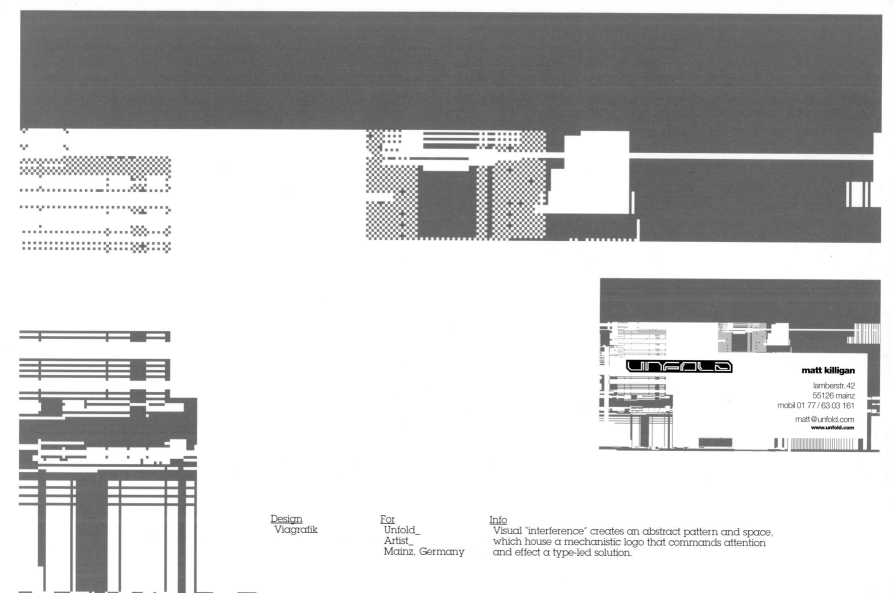

matt killigan

lamberstr. 42
55126 mainz
mobil 01 77 / 63 03 161

matt@unfold.com
www.unfold.com

Design
Viagrafik

For
Unfold_
Artist_
Mainz, Germany

Info
Visual "interference" creates an abstract pattern and space,
which house a mechanistic logo that commands attention
and effect a type-led solution.

Design
Klaus Wilhardt

For
Das Büro_
Photographers_
Copenhagen,
Denmark

Info
A duo of photographers sport colour-coded cards featuring an
iconic, gothic-inspired logo. Each partner is represented by a
colour; their letterhead is printed in each colour at either end of
the sheet. The photographers flip the paper to use the letterhead
in their personal colour.

Richard Pijs

richard.pijs@fourpack.nl

Tessa Hofman

tessa.hofman@fourpack.nl

Steve Napier

steve.napier@fourpack.nl

FoURPAcK ontwerpers

grafisch ontwerpstudio

Veemarktkade 8

5222 AE 's-Hertogenbosch

t 073 612 44 43

f 084 876 65 19

www.fourpack.nl

post@fourpack.nl

Design
Fourpack

For
Fourpack_
Designers_
's-Hertogenbosch,
The Netherlands

Info
A system inspired by the design language of stamps is used to
incorporate lo-res portraits and distinguishing icons representing
members of this multi-media design team. The mock-perforated
sections leave room for additional handwritten information.

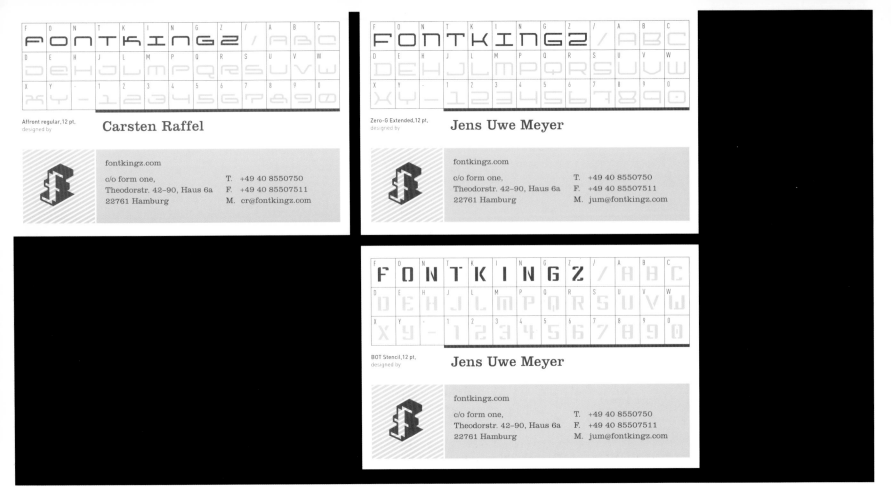

Carsten Raffel

Affront regular, 12 pt,
designed by

fontkingz.com

c/o form one,
Theodorstr. 42–90, Haus 6a
22761 Hamburg

T.   +49 40 8550750
F.   +49 40 85507511
M. cr@fontkingz.com

Jens Uwe Meyer

Zero-G Extended, 12 pt,
designed by

fontkingz.com

c/o form one,
Theodorstr. 42–90, Haus 6a
22761 Hamburg

T.   +49 40 8550750
F.   +49 40 85507511
M. jum@fontkingz.com

Jens Uwe Meyer

BOT Stencil, 12 pt,
designed by

fontkingz.com

c/o form one,
Theodorstr. 42–90, Haus 6a
22761 Hamburg

T.   +49 40 8550750
F.   +49 40 85507511
M. jum@fontkingz.com

Design
  Fontkingz

For
  Fontkingz_
  Designers_
  Hamburg, Germany

Info
  Taking the opportunity to hand out examples of fonts designed
  and produced by themselves, the partners at Fontkingz created
  a series of cards to act as a font-folio.

Design
  Jonty O'Connor

For
  Jonty O'Connor_
  Designer_
  Liverpool, UK

Info
  Including "Illustrator boxes" and a cursor, this trompe-l'oeil
  card represents a moment in the design process.

Design
Karen Jane

For
Karen Jane_
Designer_
London, UK

Info
Karen Jane calls this "an identity crisis on one small card"; she's reinterpreted various design ideas into a series of personal icons and fonts to represent herself.

KAREN JANE (MA RCA)
Design, Art Direction & Design Consultancy
Mobile: +44 (0)7973 983 953
Email: kj@karenjane.com
Web: www.karenjane.com

CRASH.
AN INFLUX PRODUCTION

JOHNNY MOY
6 TRINITY STREET. DUBLIN 2
FON. 01 6792533
FAX. 01 661 3434

MORE INFORMATION & PROPAGANDA AVAILABLE AT
WWW.INFLUXSTATE.COM.

Design
Redman AKA

For
Influx_
Record label_
Dublin, Ireland

Info
A club dedicated to playing the best new and alternative bands
and DJs from Dublin's energetic music scene, Crash was the
brainchild of club promoters Influx; this card uses elements from
the parent company's cut-up logo.

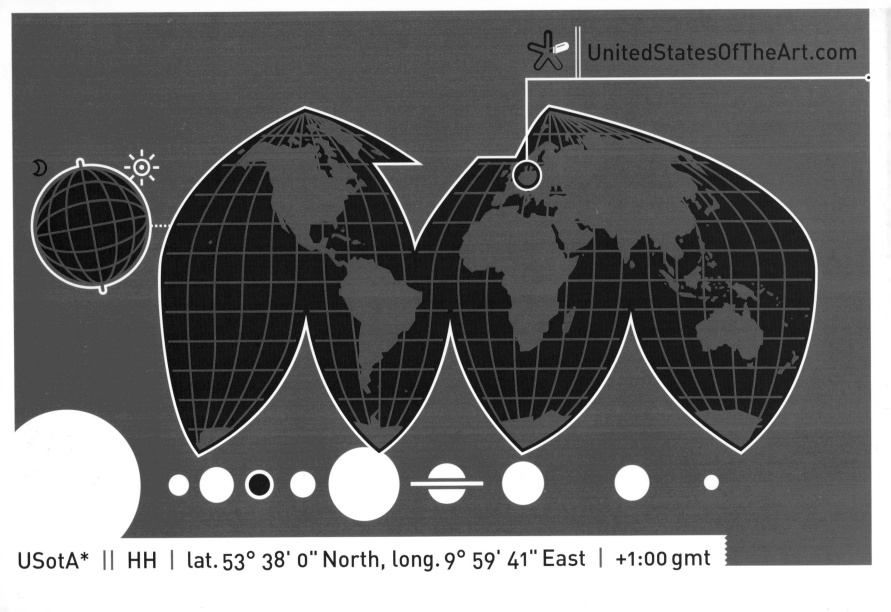

UnitedStatesOfTheArt.com

USotA* || HH | lat. 53° 38' 0" North, long. 9° 59' 41" East | +1:00 gmt

»Cargo«

Carsten Raffel,
cargo@unitedstatesoftheart.com

USOTA*

»Jum«

Jens Uwe Meyer,
jum@unitedstatesoftheart.com

USOTA*

Design
United States
of the Art

For
United States
of the Art_
Designers_
Hamburg, Germany

Info
Masters of street-inspired logo design, USOTA mix info-graphics
with a sporty colour scheme and hand-drawn tags reminiscent
of corporate name badges.

67

Design
 J6 Studios

For
 J6 Studios_
 Designers_
 Houston, USA

Info
 A beermat-style die-cut card referring to sports-team
 aesthetics makes for an exuberant, in-your-face calling card.

Design
J6 Studios

For
J6 Studios_
Designers_
Houston, USA

Info
"Old Skool" graffiti pieces and comic-book characters, fused with computerized effects, add up to Jester's approach at J6 Studios.

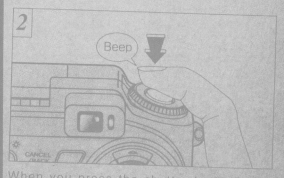

Design
Mission

For
Pål Laukli_
Photographer_
Oslo, Norway

Info
An exuberant photographer is treated to a series of cards that include his own (outspoken) quotes (in speech bubbles, naturally). Found imagery and type relating to his craft are mixed with various hand-made marks, and printed on board with fluorescent inks.

space3eindhoven
Grafische & Illustratieve Ontwerpen

Joost van der Heijden

Kerkstraat 24
5611 GJ Eindhoven

Postbus 8007
5601 KA Eindhoven

T. +31 (0)40 213 53 82
F. +31 (0)40 213 53 75
M.+31 (0)6 247 63 066
E. joost@space3.nl

Design
Space 3

For
Space 3_
Designers_
Eindhoven,
The Netherlands

Info
Displaying their individual and anarchic approach to
typography, Space 3's cards combine various mark-making
tools and styles, from shop-card marker pen to pencil scribble
(obliterating their logo).

Design/illustration
Peppered Sprout

For
Peppered Sprout_
Designers/illustrators_
Liverpool, UK

Info
A handwritten list for a favourite Indian takeaway is a treasured communication device; the giant arrow hints at another use overleaf, the cheeky addition of contact details.

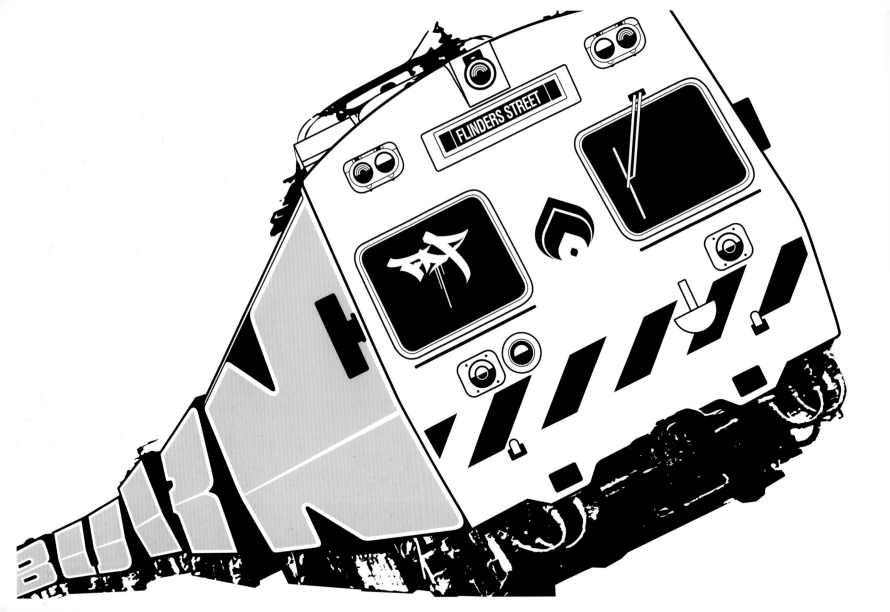

Design
Burncrew

For
Burncrew_
Designers/
clothing label_
Melbourne, Australia

Info
Maestros with minimal means – their roots are in Melbourne's
prodigious street-art scene – Burncrew capture the excitement
of urban living with a series of stark, graphic cards.

BERND URBAN
DISTRRIBUTION

KANISTER RECORDS
DOMINIKANERSTRASSE 2
D-55116 MAINZ

F +49.61 31.23 56 03 2
T +49.61 31.23 56 06

B.URBAN@KANISTER-RECORDS.DE

Design
  Viagrafik

For
  Kanister_
  Record label_
  Mainz, Germany

Info
  High-octane, optical black and white on a die-cut card,
  this heavy-duty facsimile reflects Kanister's hard-core
  musical tastes.

Design
  Paul Ayre

For
  14:59_
  Designer_
  London, UK

Info
  Designer and director Paul Ayre pairs an abstracted, pixellated portrait, printed in the subtlest varnish, with an enigmatic logo. "14:59" refers to Warhol's 15 minutes of fame quote; and the fact that "everyone working in television wants to be famous," explains Paul.

Design/illustration
Christian Petersen

For
Christian Petersen_
Graphic artist_
London, UK

Info
Pushing the possibilities of the simplest black and white print spec, this image-making designer indulges his "sex and death" fantasies with a series of uncompromising cards.

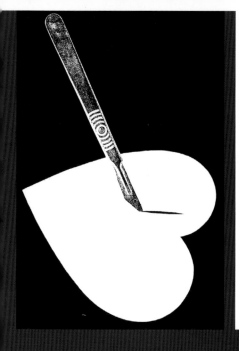

christian petersen

graphic artist

mysterycatt@hotmail.com

KISS THE BOOT

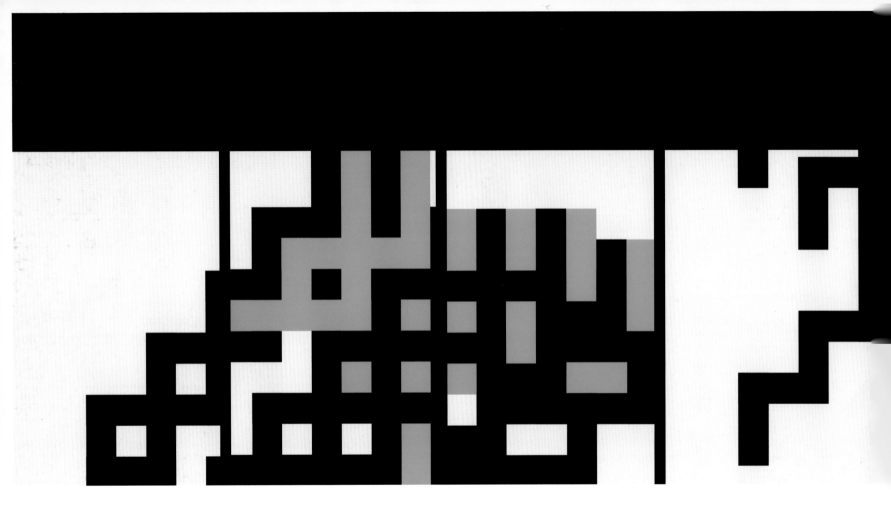

Design
Reza Abedini

For
Ati Centre_
Architects_
Teheran, Iran

Info
This series of cards for an architecture firm constructs a geometrical arrangement of squares into an illustration of built forms; the motif continues onto the reverse to house the contact information.

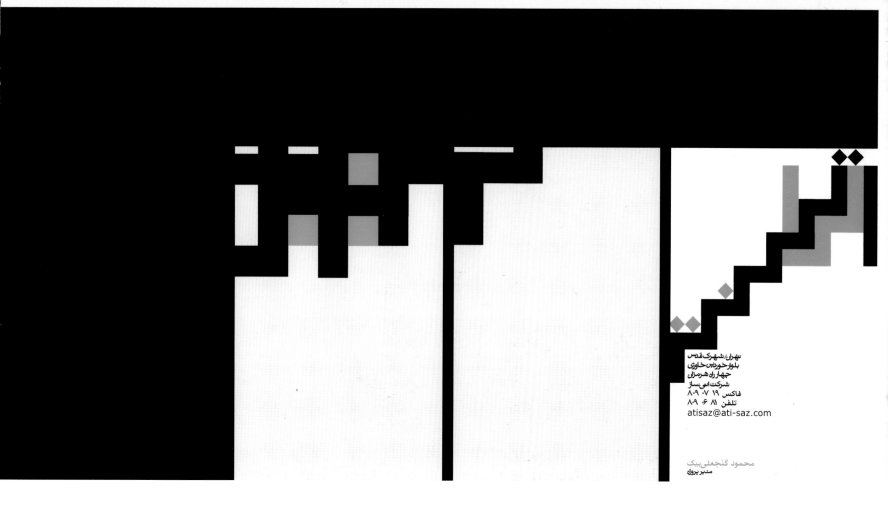

تهران/ شهرک قدس
بلوار خوردین خاوری
چهار راه هرمزان
شرکت اتی ساز
فاکس ۱۹ ۷۰ ۸۰۹
تلفن ۸۱ ۶۰ ۸۰۹
atisaz@ati-saz.com

محمود گنجعلی بیک
مدیر پروژه

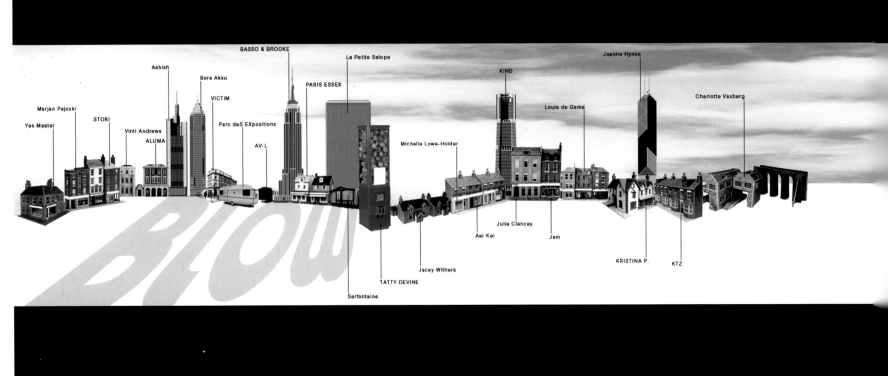

Yes Master
Marjan Pejoski
STORI
Vinti Andrews
ALUMA
Ashish
Bora Aksu
VICTIM
Parc deS EXpositions
AV-L
BASSO & BROOKE
PARIS ESSEX
La Petite Salope
Serfontaine
TATTY DEVINE
Jacey Withers
Michelle Lowe-Holder
Aei Kei
Julia Clancey
KIND
Louis de Gama
Jem
KRISTINA P.
KTZ
Joanne Hynes
Charlotte Vasberg

Design
Julianand

Photography
Ian Gillet

For
Blow_
Fashion PR_
London, UK

Info
As promoters of design talent, Blow are synonymous with
London Fashion Week. Their website is based on a scrolling,
urban skyline (with signature buildings from around the world);
this series of cards plays with the theme.

MICHAEL OLIVEIRA-SALAC
PR DIRECTOR
1ST FLOOR, 15 PERCY STREET, LONDON W1T 1DS
TEL +44 020 7436 9449   MOB 07867 900 812   FAX +44 020 7436 7027
MICHAEL@BLOW.CO.UK
WWW.BLOW.CO.UK

MICHAEL OLIVEIRA-SALAC
PR DIRECTOR
1ST FLOOR, 15 PERCY STREET, LONDON W1T 1DS
TEL +44 020 7436 9449   MOB 07867 900 812   FAX +44 020 7436 7027
MICHAEL@BLOW.CO.UK
WWW.BLOW.CO.UK

Miles Donovan Illustration
+44 (0) 7715103673 www.milesdonovan.co.uk
+44 (0) 2070339299 m@milesdonovan.co.uk

Peepshow BLACK CONVOY

Design/illustration
Miles Donovan

For
Miles Donovan_
Illustrator_
London, UK

Info
A member of illustration collective Peepshow, Miles Donovan's
work is informed by street-inspired mark-making (spray-can and
felt-tip pen) and instant media (silkscreen and stencil). His card
features a montage of the flotsam and jetsam to be found in the
urban fabric of Manhattan.

50a woodlands park road
london se10 9xd
07981551925
+44(0)2082931047
philashcroft@hotmail.com
phlashweb.co.uk

Design/illustration
Phil Ashcroft

For
Phlash_
Illustrator_
London, UK

Info
An awe-inspiring creature, shown in its natural habitat
alongside a series of wild landscapes, adds up to a high-
visibility card.

FAILE
A PLACE FOR DIALOGUE

Design/illustration
Faile

For
Faile_
Designers_
New York, USA

Info
This art and design collective are as happy working in public spaces as they are collaborating with major brands; what all projects have in common is an engagement with the processes of print, and a playful mixing of messages.

Design/illustration
Danny Sangra

For
Danny Sangra_
Illustrator_
London, UK

Info
An illustrator who is as at home painting gallery walls as he
is designing fabric prints for a fashion label, Danny uses these
cards to showcase his aesthetic, which mixes geometry and
abstraction.

FACT:01

HENRY KISSINGER: WAR CRIMINAL

FACT:02

BENEATH THE PAVEMENT LIES THE BEACH

FACT:03

Design
 Them

Illustrations
 Miles Donovan_
 Shepard Fairey_
 Oscar Wilson_
 Jo Ratcliffe_

For
 FACT_
 Magazine_
 London, UK

Info
 A new set of business cards based on current themes and
 visuals accompanies each issue of FACT, a magazine for
 enthusiasts of music on vinyl. Employing upfront aesthetics
 and no-nonsense copy, these cards hint at the energy and
 attitude of a publication that is fighting back against
 encroaching digitization.

Illustrations
Trevor Jackson_
Barry McGee_
2sickbastards_
Os Gemeos
Cut Copy

FACT:10

AUTUMN 2005. FREE

FACT:11

WINTER 2005. FREE

FACT:

SEAN BIDDER IS THE EDITOR
OF FACT MAGAZINE

FACT MAGAZINE
VINYL FACTORY PUBLISHING LIMITED
BASEMENT STUDIO
45 FOUBERTS PLACE
LONDON W1F 7QH
SEAN.BIDDER@VINYLFACTORY.CO.UK
WWW.FACTMAGAZINE.CO.UK
TELEPHONE: 0207 025 1386

Design
Neasden Control
Centre

For
Neasden Control
Centre_
Designers_
London, UK

Info
Anarchic mark-makers and masters of cut-and-paste, NCC are
irreverent iconoclasts who are earning a fast-growing reputation
for their uncompromising aesthetic. Their cards are hand-made
or batch-produced, and display signs of both dizzying speed and
obsessive attention to detail.

NEASDEN CONTROL CENTRE

SMITH IS OPERATING IN THE AREA

2
1 2 3

EMAIL:

www.neasdencontrolcentre.com

NEA DENɕ ?

BUSINESS   TO

HTTP://NEASDEN
WWW.
CONTROL
CENTRE
.COM

make sure your are with friends to celebrate

STEP02°POLITICS

ENJOY!POLITICS

Design
Wuff Design

For
Enjoy Politics_
Magazine_
Frankfurt, Germany

Info
Black silhouettes and type are overprinted in magenta; noughts
and crosses denote a game while the imagery suggests something
more violent is occurring, perhaps where play and real life collide;
the reverse of the card spells out the magazine's title.

make sure your team is going to win

SHOUT 1 POLITICS

ENJOY!POLITICS

MICHAELA KESSLER
CONTACT@ENJOY-POLITICS.DE

make sure your are with friends to celebrate

ENJOY 2 POLITICS

ENJOY!POLITICS

PUNK FILMS™
パンク　フィルム

PUNK FILMS™
パンク　フィルム

PUNK FILMS™
パンク　フィルム

**Punk Films
パンク　フィルム
Mark Logue
マーク、ローグ
Director
ディレクター**

Unit 2A Queens Studio 121 Salusbury Road London NW6 6RG UK
M +44 (0)7970 004 680 T +44 (0)20 7372 4474 D +44 (0)20 7644 6594
E mark@punk.uk.com www.punk.uk.com

Design
 David Bowden
 Zip Design

For
 Punk Films_
 Moving visuals
 company_
 London, UK

Info
 Eight variations on camouflage grace the fronts of this series
 of cards for a company that produces moving visuals. A patch
 of white on the black ground of the reverse provides space for
 handwritten information.

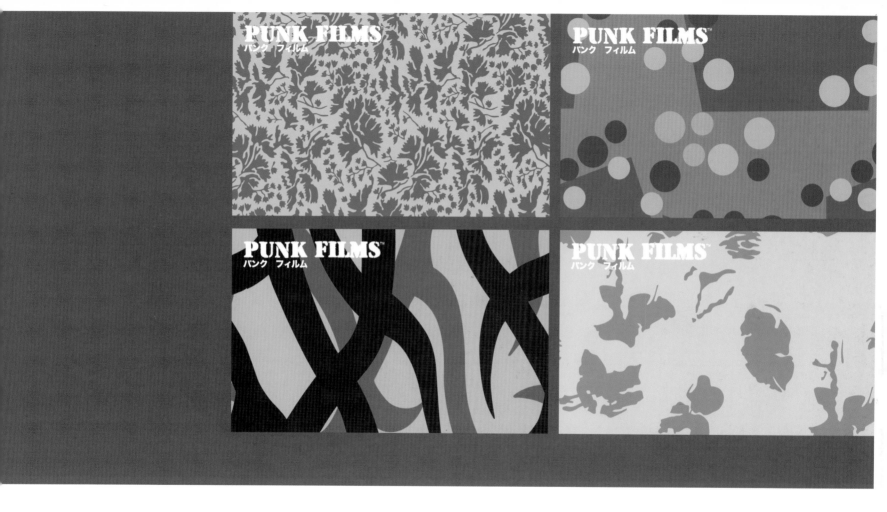

Design
Staple Design

For
Staple Design_
Designers_
New York, USA

Info
Combining the edginess of various camouflage patterns with
engravings of American national heroes, more usually found on
dollar bills, this design company borrows a degree of gravitas
from tradition while subverting the supposed neutrality of overly
familiar faces.

 http://www.stapledesign.com/

a positive social contagion.

$tpl

Aiko Company Building Tokyo
Aiko
Furi Furi #202 Akasaka-ku
2-1-10 Shibuya-ku
Sendagaya
151005

Yoshimi Nasu
Yoshimi Nasu Company Building Tokyo
Furi Furi Akasaka-ku
Furi #202
2-1-10 Shibuya
Sendagaya
151

Designer
Miki Kobayashi
Designer Company Building Tokyo
Miki Kobayashi Akasaka-ku
Furi Furi #202 Shibuya
2-1-10
Sendagaya
151

Creative Director
Creative Tei Company Building
Furi Furi Akasaka-ku Tokyo
yosuke Company Tokyo

Design
Furi Furi Company

For
Furi Furi Company_
Designers_
Tokyo, Japan

Info
A super-friendly, smiley logo is turned into a circular
card, with buzzy colour-coded versions for each staff member.

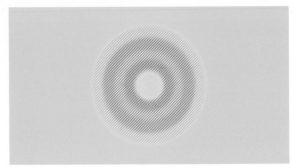

PLAYMANAGEMENT
NORDSTRANDVEIEN 5 1170 OSLO NORWAY
TEL +47 2229 2505 **FAX** +47 2229 2504
E-MAIL PLAY@PLAYMANAGEMENT.COM
WWW.PLAYMANAGEMENT.COM

Design
Mission

For
Play_
Music management_
Oslo, Norway

Info
Mixing yellow with blue using the finest of lines, this series
of cards literally "plays" with two colours and the infinite
possibilities of stripes.

Design
Neil Edwards

For
Mr. Edwards_
Designer_
Sydney, Australia

Info
A constant collector of imagery and copy-lines, Neil Edwards
uses and reuses familiar icons in unexpected combinations.
His card, for alter ego Mr.Edwards, combines weather-map
graphics and humorous faces to make you laugh.

Design
 Neil Bowan
 Zip Design

For
 Wizzard_
 Advertising agency_
 London, UK

Info
 A series of blue skies populated with clouds resembling "think" bubbles, complete with idealized rays of sunshine: this series of cards is deceptively simple, concentrating as it does on the most subtle of differences.

KEMISTRY

Graham McCallum / Partner

Mobile Contact:
+44(0) 7870 698 538

Kemistry 43 Charlotte Road Shoreditch London EC2A 3PD
Email graham@kemistry.co.uk Web www.kemistry.co.uk
Telephone +44(0) 20 7729 3636 Fax +44(0) 20 7749 2760

Ricky Churchill / Partner

Mobile Contact:
+44(0) 7973 762 687

Kemistry 43 Charlotte Road Shoreditch London EC2A 3PD
Email ricky@kemistry.co.uk Website www.kemistry.co.uk
Telephone +44(0) 20 7729 3636 Fax +44(0) 20 7749 2760

Dan Witchell / Creative Director

Mobile Contact:
+44(0) 7956 101 119

Kemistry 43 Charlotte Road Shoreditch London EC2A 3PD
Email dan@kemistry.co.uk Website www.kemistry.co.uk
Telephone +44(0) 20 7729 3636 Fax +44(0) 20 7749 2760

Steve Hooley / Interactive Design

Kemistry 43 Charlotte Road Shoreditch London EC2A 3PD
Email steve@kemistry.co.uk Web www.kemistry.co.uk
Telephone +44(0) 20 7729 3636 Fax +44(0) 20 7749 2760

Design
Kemistry

For
Kemistry_
Designers_
London, UK

Info
Every member of this design consultancy has been allocated
an individual pairing of multi-coloured discs, the pseudo-
scientific significance of which remains to be determined.

Guy Hewitt / Marketing Director

Mobile Contact:
+44(0) 7774 120 002

Kemistry 43 Charlotte Road Shoreditch London EC2A 3PD
Email guy@kemistry.co.uk Website www.kemistry.co.uk
Telephone +44(0) 20 7729 3636 Fax +44(0) 20 7749 2760

Mark Gardner / Senior Designer

Kemistry 43 Charlotte Road Shoreditch London EC2A 3PD
Email mark@kemistry.co.uk Website www.kemistry.co.uk
Telephone +44(0) 20 7729 3636 Fax +44(0) 20 7749 2760

Helen Barrett / Project Manager

Mobile Contact:
+44(0) 7958 710 560

Kemistry 43 Charlotte Road Shoreditch London EC2A 3PD
Email helen@kemistry.co.uk Web www.kemistry.co.uk
Telephone +44(0) 20 7729 3636 Fax +44(0) 20 7749 2760

Sam Glynne / Public Relations

Kemistry 43 Charlotte Road Shoreditch London EC2A 3PD
Email sam@kemistry.co.uk Website www.kemistry.co.uk
Telephone +44(0) 20 7729 3636 Fax +44(0) 20 7749 2760

Isabel McCallum

Kemistry 43 Charlotte Road Shoreditch London EC2A 3PD
Email chilled_shots@msn.com Web www.kemistry.co.uk
Telephone +55(0) 21 3873 4640 Fax +44(0) 20 7749 2760

Marc Ortmans / Project Director

Mobile Contact:
+44(0) 7780 697 700

Kemistry 43 Charlotte Road Shoreditch London EC2A 3PD
Email marc@kemistry.co.uk Website www.kemistry.co.uk
Telephone +44(0) 20 7729 3636 Fax +44(0) 20 7749 2760

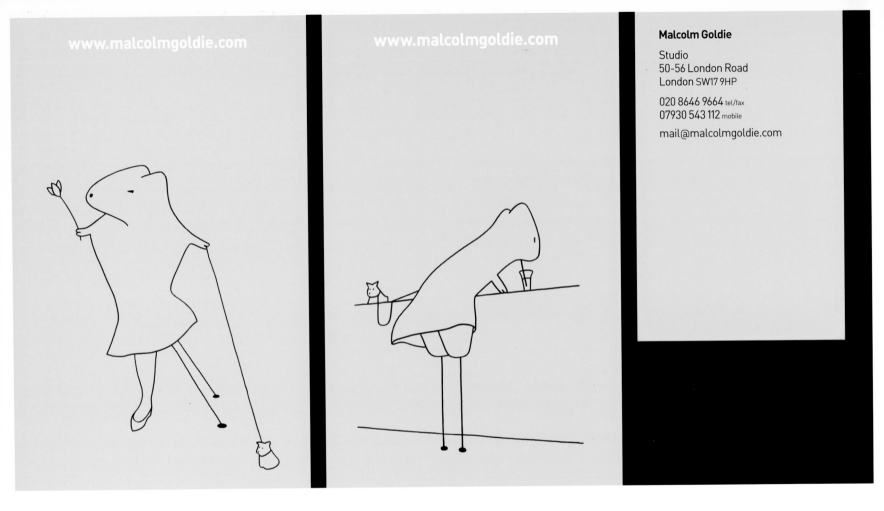

Malcolm Goldie

Studio
50-56 London Road
London SW17 9HP

020 8646 9664 tel/fax
07930 543 112 mobile

mail@malcolmgoldie.com

Design/illustration
Malcolm Goldie

For
Malcolm Goldie_
Illustrator_
London, UK

Info
Idiosyncratic designer, image-maker and musician Malcolm
Goldie's canary-yellow cards feature drawings of cute, mutant
rodents, confidently rendered in the finest of lines and posed in
various enigmatic situations.

PETE FOWLER

Monsterism Island

studio +44 (0)20 7729 4060
mobile +44 (0)7958 900961

fowler.p@virgin.net   8-10 Rhoda Street
www.monsterism.net   London E2 7EF UK

Design/illustration
Pete Fowler

For
Pete Fowler_
Designer/illustrator_
London, UK

Info
A prodigious creator of crazy characters, Pete Fowler's universe of vinyl figures, aka Monsterism Island, is fast invading the desk and shelf space of grown-up kids worldwide. Pete's card features a typically sinister but surreal figment of his imagination.

john hersey

duckface inc

character design
illustration
duckface.com
hersey.com
t 415 302 9401

<u>Design/illustration</u>
John Hersey

<u>For</u>
Duckface Inc_
Illustrator_
San Francisco, USA

<u>Info</u>
Multi-media illustrator and creature creator John Hersey's card
is die-cut and convincingly organic. Designed for a trade show,
to hang from a lanyard with your ID badge, "it's funny and
always gets a good reaction, everyone wants one," explains John.

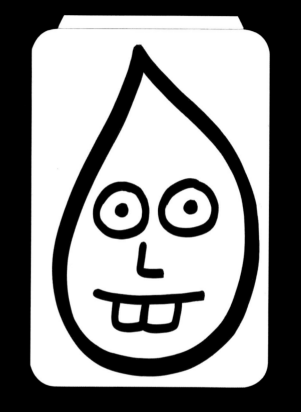

Design
Dave Warnke

For
Dave_
Designer/illustrator_
San Francisco, USA

Info
Prodigious sticker artist, illustrator, painter and creature creator
Dave conjures up a myriad of characters with the simplest of
means – black line on white ground – to grace his gallery of
business cards.

muju@mujuworld.co.uk

muju
www.mujuworld.co.uk

Design
Muju

For
Muju_
Art label_
Brighton, UK

Info
Hand-drawn Muju-monsters live in a playful world of friendly plants and animals; this series of cards hints at Muju's virtuosity in creating T-shirts, bags, toys, accessories and artworks.

Design/illustration
Harmen Liemburg

For
Harmen Liemburg_
Designer_
Amsterdam,
The Netherlands

Info
Declaring that "saying hello is my business", Harmen Liemburg silkscreen-prints cards, overlaying colours and metallic inks, and then gives them to friends, family and clients as a means of "communicating and exchanging ideas with like-minded souls". Basing his practice on "Surimono", the Japanese woodblock tradition of combining poetry and imagery to convey personal messages, Harmen points out that "the value of these small prints lies in the time and energy invested".

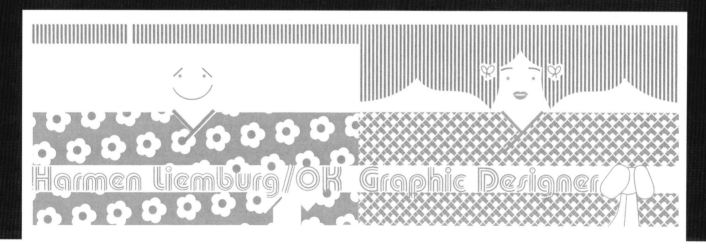

Harmen Liemburg/OK Graphic Designer

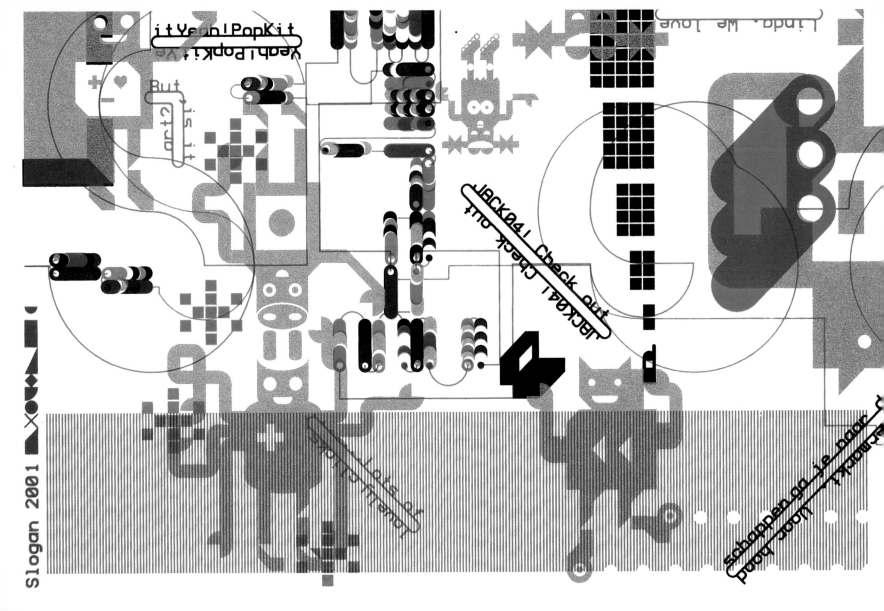

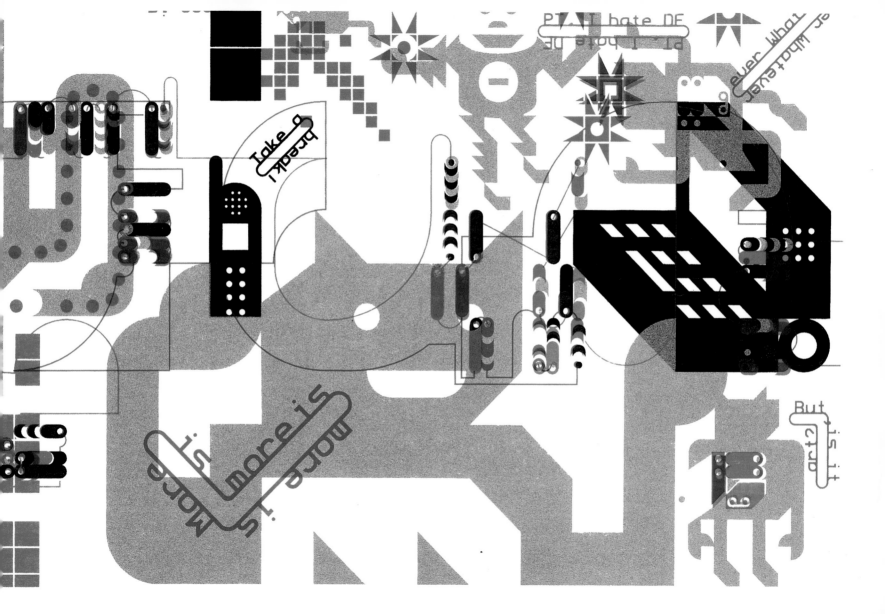

MOBILE: (+44) 77 9048 6659
EMAIL: ORKO@HOUSEOFORKO.COM
WEB: WWW.HOUSEOFORKO.COM

Design/illustration
Orko

For
Orko_
Illustrator_
London, UK

Info
The alter ego of an illustrator and designer, Orko gets up to mischief
in a world of weird, wired characters and street-style adventures.

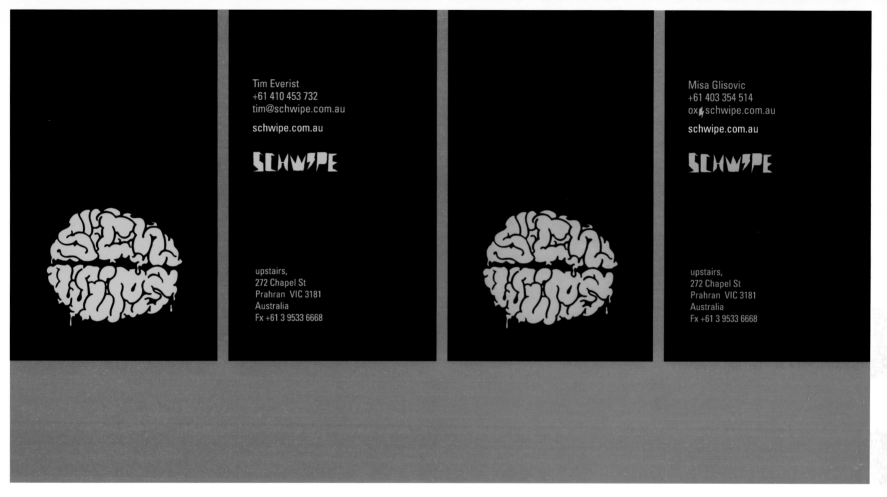

Tim Everist
+61 410 453 732
tim@schwipe.com.au

schwipe.com.au

SCHWIPE

upstairs,
272 Chapel St
Prahran VIC 3181
Australia
Fx +61 3 9533 6668

Misa Glisovic
+61 403 354 514
ox schwipe.com.au

schwipe.com.au

SCHWIPE

upstairs,
272 Chapel St
Prahran VIC 3181
Australia
Fx +61 3 9533 6668

Design
Tim Everist

For
Schwipe_
Clothing label_
Melbourne, Australia

Info
Two sides of the brain make up "Schwipe", a clothing line
that revels in radical prints and in-your-face graphics.

Design/illustration
Zinc

For
Malita Machina_
Designers_
Buenos Aires,
Argentina

Info
Mechanistic, digital, obsessive and hand-drawn; a pair
of cards for these designers explore some aspects of their
craft and lifestyle.

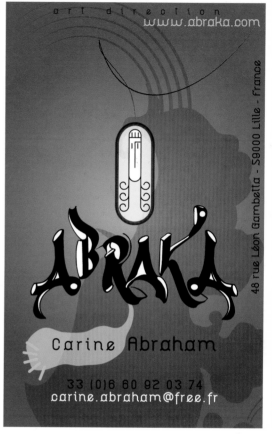

Design/illustration
Carine Abraham

For
 Abraka_
 Designer_
 Lille, France

Info
A designer who isn't afraid to take a line for a walk. Combining sensuous imagery, photography and intense colours, Carine Abraham's cards include "self-portrait" icons, in various illustrative styles.

Design
  Andy Sargent

For
  Seven-nine_
  Designer_
  Melbourne,
  Australia

Info
  A graphic designer with a gothic sense of humour, Andy
  Sargent's visual vocabulary of spider's webs, haunted houses
  and dead trees translates into his seasonal clothing collection;
  his personal stationery mutates to echo new themes.

Design
Manuel Duboe

For
Duboe Design_
Designer_
Buenos Aires,
Argentina
London, UK

Info
Dividing his time between London and Buenos Aires, this
designer produces two, colour-coded versions of his card,
one for each city.

MANUEL DUBOÉ

WWW.DUBOEDESIGN.COM
ART DIRECTION . DESIGN . ILLUSTRATION

E: MANUEL@DUBOEDESIGN.COM
M: +44 (0)7792 780 888

19 WILLOUGHBY HOUSE
REARDON PATH
LONDON, E1W 2PQ

MANUEL DUBOE

DIRECCION DE ARTE . DISEÑO . ILUSTRACION

AVELLANEDA 1489 - CP 1712
BUENOS AIRES
ARGENTINA
TEL +54 11 4 343 1207

San•jai Bha•na (san'jé bä'nä)

n. [< Hind.] 1973- ;
Illustrator & Designer
1. possesses exceptional creative talent.
2. highly proficient in various artistic mediums [see virtuoso]

www.sanjaibhana.com

Design/illustration
Sanjai Bhana

For
Sanjai Bhana_
Illustrator_
Toronto, Canada

Info
Indulging in some "Old Skool" glamour, this illustrator uses a business card to show off serious skills.

Design
Zookeeper

For
64 Design_
Designers_
Serres-Morlaas,
France

Info
Exuberant, multi-layered, eye-catching: these
cards demonstrate a playful attitude to design.

Design/illustration
Simone Legno

For
Designergokko_
Tokidoki_
Illustrator/designer/
fashion brand_
Rome, Italy
Los Angeles, USA

Info
Designer, illustrator and "brand" Simone has various
incarnations and is the creator of an imaginary world of cute
and sexy beings. The name of his T-shirt and accessories label,
Designergokko, refers to the Japanese word "gokko", meaning
"to play at dress-up".

simone legno
simone@tokidoki.it

u.s. mob * +001 310 435 27 95
italy mob *+39 349 32 78 311
*personal site
www.designergokko.it
*brand (los angeles - CA)
www.tokidoki.it
*design studio (roma - Italy)
www.vianet.it

Rian Hughes

Device
2 Blake Mews
Kew Gardens
Richmond
TW9 3GA
UK

Telephone: 020 8896 0626
Telephone: +44(0)20 8896 0626
Facsimile: 020 8439 9080
Mobile: 07979 60 22 72
Web: www.rianhughes.com
Font sales: www.devicefonts.co.uk
Email: rian@rianhughes.com
AOL: rianhughes@aol.com

Design/illustration
Rian Hughes

For
Rian Hughes_
Designer/illustrator_
London, UK

Info
An accomplished designer of marques, typefaces and illustrated worlds, Rian's own cards feature a mini-gallery of his playful creations.

bimbo
DELUXE

376 Brunswick Street
Fitzroy 3065 Victoria Australia

Tel +61 3 9419 8600
Fax +61 3 9419 8210

Email bimbo@bimbodeluxe.com.au
www.bimbodeluxe.com.au

Design
Alter

For
Bimbo Deluxe_
Bar_
Melbourne,
Australia

Info
An irony-laden name for a bar, with a card featuring that
perennial cultural icon, the Kewpie doll; Alter mix "cute"
and "vamp" to create "bimbo".

no more than a trained
CHIMP
David Horwood illustrator

Design/illustration
David Horwood

For
David Horwood_
Designer/illustrator_
London, UK

Info
In his "early days as an illustrator", David (nicknamed The Chimp) handed out hand-drawn cards, each one an original.

141

AKIN AKINSIKU

ART DIRECTOR

NICKELODEON UK
15-18
RATHBONE PLACE
LONDON
W1T 1HU

E: AKIN.AKINSIKU @ NIC
KELODEON.CO.UK
T: 020 7462 1032
WWW.NICK.CO.UK

NICKELOT

GEOFF PARSONS

DESIGNER

NICKELODEON UK
15-18
RATHBONE PLACE
LONDON
W1T 1HU

E: GEOFF.PARSONS @ NI
CKELODEON.CO.UK
T: 020 7462 1073
WWW.NICK.CO.UK

NICKELOT

Art direction
  Akin Akinsiku_
  Paul Ayre

Design
  Paul Ayre_
  Rohat Cellali-Sik

Typography
  Jon Abbott_
  Neville Brody_
  Declan Brody_
  Research Studios

For
  Nickelodeon_
  TV channel_
  London, UK

Info
Based on the premise "give a child a crayon and they'll start
drawing", these cards feature self-penned portraits by
Nickelodeon staff. With type design by Neville Brody and his
seven-year-old son, Declan, the paper-based identity reflects
the onscreen look of this kid-friendly TV channel.

LAI MARSH
3D DESIGNER

NICKELODEON UK
15-18
RATHBONE PLACE
LONDON
W1T 1HU

E: LAI.MARSH @ NICKEL
ODEON.CO.UK
T: 020 7462 1071
WWW.NICK.CO.UK

NICKELOD

MARK WARBROOK
SENIOR ON AIR DESIGNER

NICKELODEON UK
15-18
RATHBONE PLACE
LONDON
W1T 1HU

E: MARKWA @ NICKELOD
EON.CO.UK
T: 020 7462 1032
M: 07946 545141
WWW.NICK.CO.UK

NICKELOD

ROHAT CELLALI-SIK
OFF AIR DESIGNER

NICKELODEON UK
15-18
RATHBONE PLACE
LONDON
W1T 1HU

E: ROHAT @ NICKELODEO
N.CO.UK
T: 020 7462 1035
WWW.NICK.CO.UK

NICKELOD

Some Pro

All The Shit I

Issue 01 / Winter '05 / Lim

<u>Design/illustration</u>
Mark James

<u>For</u>
Mark James_
Designer/illustrator_
London, UK

<u>Info</u>
Instead of a card simply directing interested parties to a website,
Mark James decided to make an ever-changing mini-portfolio
housed in a box by collating stickers, die-cut cards, logos for
his own "sub-brands" and junk food-inspired artworks. The box
features a cast-metal pin, while one card includes a scratch-off
panel – which people are reluctant to remove!

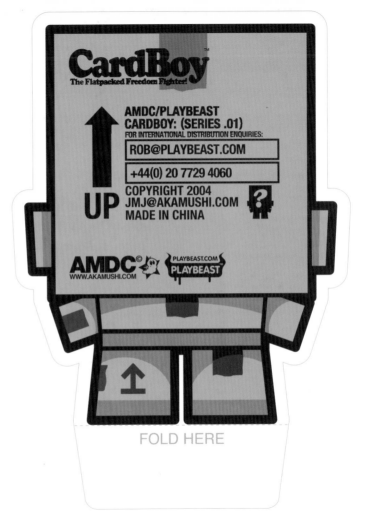

Cell: +44 [0] 7747 777994

Mail: jmj@akamushi.com

Issue: 001

AKAMUSHI.COM

Design/illustration
Spencer Wilson

For
Spencer Wilson_
Illustrator_
London, UK

Info
An alternative aesthetic for Spencer, this time foregrounding
his illustration work; cute and comic characters and creatures
populate his universe.

Design/illustration
Mick Marston

For
Mick Marston_
Illustrator_
Sheffield, UK

Info
An illustrator with a multitude of styles, Mick montages cute,
quirky, bizarre and surreal images to "acid-tinged" textures;
he's particularly cruel to animals (but not in real life!).

東京Ⓐリス
（トウキョウアリス）

〒150-0045
渋谷区神泉町 2・1, D 202

tel&fax 0334612403
ケータイ 09098459139
http://www.tokyoalice.com
alice@illustar.com

Design/illustration
Tokyo Alice

For
Tokyo Alice_
Illustrator_
Tokyo, Japan

Info
Self-styled "Punk Illustar" Tokyo Alice uses these cards to show off her aesthetic and to introduce a cast of characters, from cheeky chipmunks to angelic kimono-clad girls; welcome to Alice's world.

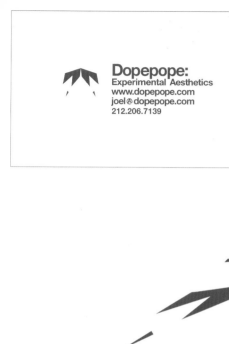

Dopepope:
Experimental Aesthetics
www.dopepope.com
joel@dopepope.com
212.206.7139

Design
  Dopepope

For
  Dopepope_
  Designer_
  New York, USA

Info
  This design and clothing label, with its tag line of "Experimental
  Aesthetics", revels in mechanistic/techno/space-age imagery;
  cards feature fantasy devices and slick logos.

Eelco van den Berg
'Artwork pleasure'

+31 (0)6 25 413 403 · www.eelcovandenberg.com · eelco@eelcovandenberg.com

Design/illustration
Eelco van den Berg

For
Eelco van den Berg_
Illustrator_
Rotterdam,
The Netherlands

Info
Fantasies of mechanistic robot women, teamed with demonic
fauna, display Eelco's illustration skills, in this series of highly
decorative, overtly erotic cards.

Eelco van den Berg

'Artwork pleasure'

+31 (0)6 25 413 403 · www.eelcovandenberg.com · eelco@eelcovandenberg.com

Eelco van den Berg

'Artwork pleasure'

+31 (0)6 25 413 403 · www.eelcovandenberg.com · eelco@eelcovandenberg.com

Design/illustration
 Fraser Davidson_
 Adam Deeley_
 Felix Kiessling_
 Paddy Mills_
 Kate Moross_
 Richard Moross_
 William Rowe

For
 PleasureCards_
 Personal contact
 cards_
 London, UK

Info
 A new venture in Internet communication: designs for business
 cards are uploaded by graphic designers and illustrators, the
 public choose their favourites and receive a set of personalized
 cards by post. The possibilities are endless, while the format
 remains the same, which is ideal for updating, mixing and
 matching.

155

Design/Illustration
Steve Wilson

For
Steve Wilson_
Illustrator_
London, UK

Info
Utilizing his business cards as a mini-portfolio, Steve Wilson showcases his proficiency across a range of image-making techniques. By focusing on portraiture, he's able to push the requirements of representation to the limit while retaining an element of recognition.

Steve Wilson
www.wilson2000.com
Agent:www.pearcestoner.com
Tel:07939 216666
steve@wilson2000.com

Design/illustration
Nick Purser

For
Nick Purser_
Designer/illustrator_
London, UK

Info
A versatile practitioner, Nick Purser uses these cards
to demonstrate his virtuosity as an illustrator.

Lee Ford Illustration/www.leeford.net

Design/illustration
Lee Ford

For
Lee Ford_
Illustrator_
London, UK

Info
Mixing sharply delineated blocks of colour, subtly worked-over
textures and various methods of collaging, Lee Ford's cards hint
at the versatility of his pen.

Mielo

Design/Illustration

Katharina Leuzinger
T 07813 919 442   E katleuzinger@tiscali.co.uk   www.mielo.co.uk

Design/illustration
Katharina
Leuzinger

For
Mielo_
Designer/illustrator_
London, UK

Info
A skilled renderer, Katharina Leuzinger's work is also
exuberantly colourful. For these business cards, however, she
converts her imagery into monotone drawings, printed onto
heavy, creamy stock, so as to create a series from a selection
of previous work.

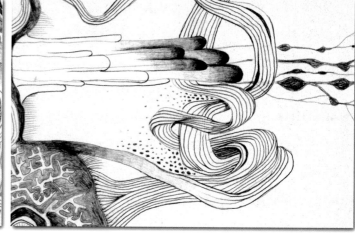

Mielo

Katharina Leuzinger

T 07813 919 442   E katleuzinger@tiscali.co.uk   www.mielo.co.uk

Each card repeats:

KamTang
18 Southwell Road London SE5 9PG
TEL/FAX +44 (0)20 77371113
www.kamtang.com mail@kamtang.com

Design/illustration
Kam Tang

For
Kam Tang_
Designer/illustrator_
London, UK

Info
Precision illustrator Kam Tang creates intricate worlds with fine lines; this idealized, fantasy creature takes on different personalities depending on the print colours.

phuturelondon

Irene Ong
General Manager

plondon@singnet.com.sg
www.phuturelondon.com

2 Jalan Rajah #06-06 Golden Wall Building Singapore 329134
T (065) 62534977 F (065) 62534923

<u>Design</u>
Niche

<u>For</u>
Phuture London_
Fashion, textiles and
retail company_
Singapore

<u>Info</u>
Created for designers, manufacturers and retailers of directional
but feminine fashion, this card features flora and fauna
rendered in contemporary hues.

164

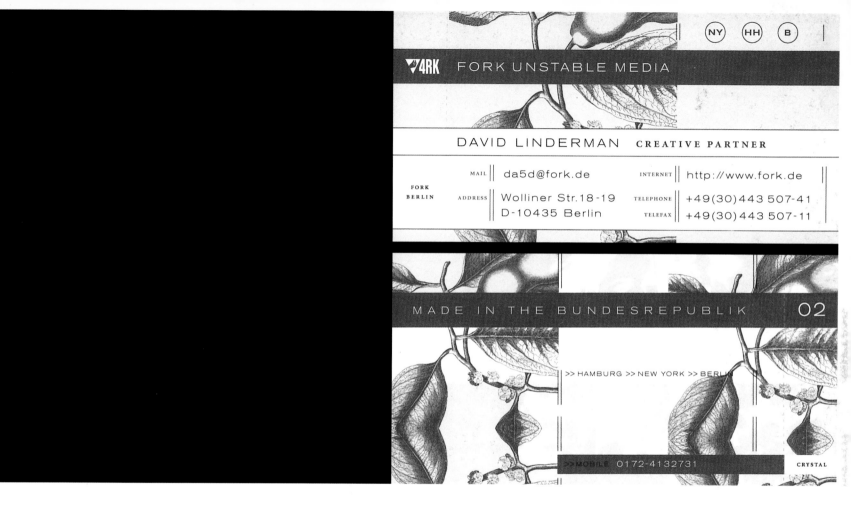

Design
Marius Fahrner_
David Linderman

For
Fork Unstable Media_
Designers_
Berlin/Hamburg,
Germany
New York, USA

Info
Establishing a rigid grid over a lush, organic illustration, an
"abstract interpretation of the Garden of Eden" complete with
Adam and Eve, these business cards function for all three studio
locations: New York, Hamburg and Berlin.

intramuros
international design magazine

Design
June

For
Intramuros_
Magazine_
Paris, France

Info
Icons of furniture, graphic and product design are interwoven, in silhouette to create an emblematic tableau, depicting the breadth of this stylish design magazine's remit. Each staff member is represented by an instantly recognizable design classic.

intramuros
29 rue de meaux
79019 paris
http://www.intramuros.fr

mina bui
publicité développement
33 (0)1 42 03 95 94
minabui@intramuros.fr

intramuros
29 rue de meaux
79019 paris
http://www.intramuros.fr

julien crouigneau
directeur artistique
33 (6) 81 43 34 83
julien@designjune.com

intramuros
29 rue de meaux
79019 paris
http://www.intramuros.fr

chantal hamaide
directrice de la rédaction
33 (0)1 42 03 95 95
info@intramuros.fr

Design
 Bureau Ludwig

For
 Villa Athletico_
 Clothing label_
 Berlin, Germany

Info
 A print-based street-fashion label, celebrating pop-culture icons,
 is treated to a strong, graphic card incorporating stripes and a
 fade-out.

we are fallon
67-69 beak street london W1F 9SW
t +44 (0) 207 534 0677
f +44 (0) 207 494 9130
www.fallon.co.uk
i'm simone wagener designer
simone.wagener@fallon.co.uk
m +44 (0) 7780 601 472

Stuff I remember about Simone:

<u>Design</u>
 Richard Flintham_
 Andy McLeod_
 Simone Wagener

<u>Illustration</u>
 Roger Gorridge_
 Roger Kent

<u>For</u>
 Fallon_
 Advertising agency_
 London, UK

<u>Info</u>
 A range of boldly illustrated cards, mixing wildlife and technology, was created for this cutting-edge advertising agency following the same approach that it uses for its own clients. This guarantees that they "stand out from the crowd".

Design/illustration
Karen Ingram

For
Karen Ingram_
Illustrator_
Brooklyn, USA

Info
Super-refined and multi-layered illustrations create a sumptuous
series of cards. Each is hand-numbered and limited to an edition
of 500; a true artwork in miniature.

Karen S. Ingram
Hand

www.krening.com
www.kareningram.com
karen@krening.com

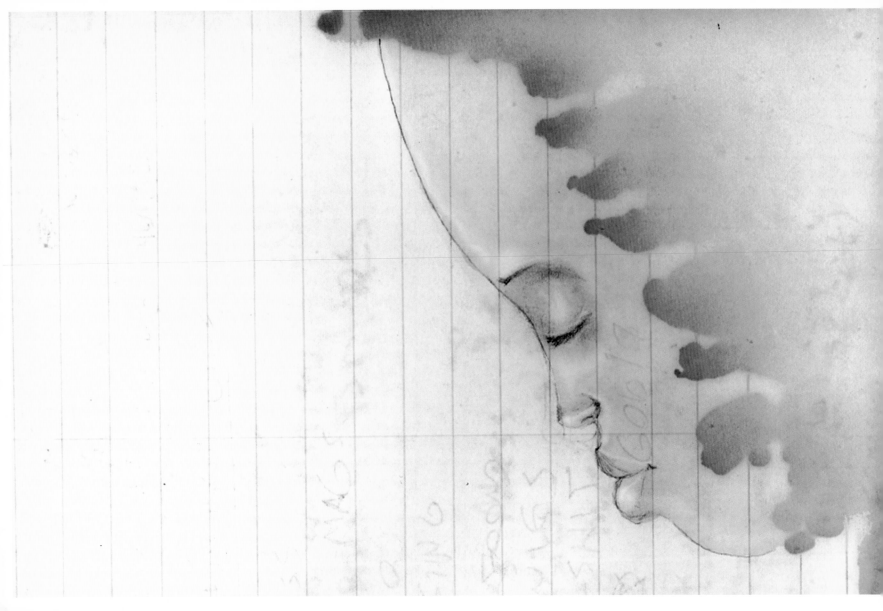

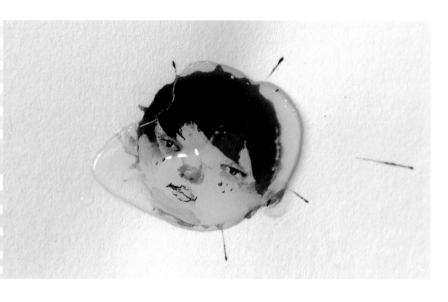

Design/illustration
David Choe

For
David Choe_
Artist_
San José, USA

Info
Making his cards a fraction larger than average so as to stand out but still fit a wallet, David Choe presents different sides of his personality via two designs. The gold ink drawing of a woman on red card stock versus the simian ape in silver on black stock, representing feminine and masculine respectively – David will choose which to give out in any situation. His name alone is embossed on the reverse, challenging you to discover his contact details. Occasionally, if he finds a cache of interesting paper stock, David will hand-paint "a bunch of tiny cards for special people".

Design/illustration
Peppered Sprout

For
Peppered Sprout_
Designers/illustrators_
Liverpool, UK

Info
With this card, illustrators and art directors Peppered Sprout
demonstrate that their drawing skills are only one part of the
equation; real life closely observed translates into unique
conceptual thinking.

STOP FOLLOWING ME productions

STOP FOLLOWING ME PRODUCTIONS

DIRECTOR (CEO) BEN WOLFINSOHN ADDRESS**1228 WASHINGTON AVE, SANTA MONICA CA 90403** PHONE **310 393 2704** EMAIL **BENWOLFINSOHN@STOPFOLLOWINGME.COM** WEB **STOPFOLLOWINGME.COM**

Design/illustration
Ben Wolfinsohn

For
Stop Following Me
Productions_
Filmmaker_
Santa Monica, USA

Info
An independent filmmaker who produces his own projects, Ben Wolfinsohn created a suitably ad-hoc card, using ruled notepaper and a hand-drawn illustration, reminiscent of cliff-hanging cable-car scenes in great movies.

COLLECTION LAMBERT

5, RUE VIOLETTE 84000 AVIGNON
RENSEIGNEMENTS : 0490.165.620

COLLECTION LAMBERT

5, RUE VIOLETTE 84000 AVIGNON
RENSEIGNEMENTS : 0490.165.620

COLLECTION LAMBERT

5, RUE VIOLETTE 84000 AVIGNON
RENSEIGNEMENTS : 0490.165.620

COLLECTION LAMBERT

5, RUE VIOLETTE 84000 AVIGNON
RENSEIGNEMENTS : 0490.165.620

COLLECTION LAMBERT

5, RUE VIOLETTE 84000 AVIGNON
RENSEIGNEMENTS : 0490.165.620

Design
Antoine+Manuel

For
Collection Lambert_
Art gallery_
Avignon, France

Info
Part of an evolving series of stickers featuring new exhibitions
and rendered in an approachable illustrative style, these image-
cards are collected by visitors and displayed around town.

Design
  Canefantasma
  Studio

For
  Canefantasma
  Studio_
  Designers_
  Siena, Italy

Info
  These accomplished image-makers, who produce advertising and graphics for corporate and cultural clients, as well as personal work that includes book design and print-making, have created a card series from found and altered imagery, focusing on spiritual and political subject matter.

COCK'S BONES FOUND IN A ROMAN URN AT LEWES, BY
DR. GIDEON MANTELL, IN 1814

een an

Design/illustration
Reuben Raffael

For
Zoltron Industries_
Designers/shop_
San Francisco, USA

Info
A hundred-year-old album of ancestral photographs made a chance encounter with a book about chickens on Reuben Raffael's scanner, where he merged the non-smiling family members with "The Fairest Fowl", and printed them onto suitably stiff recycled board as business cards. Reuben explains: "I decided to sacrifice the honour of my ancestors' dignity and digitally alter our genetic history into what I always thought our family's true calling was… circus freaks."

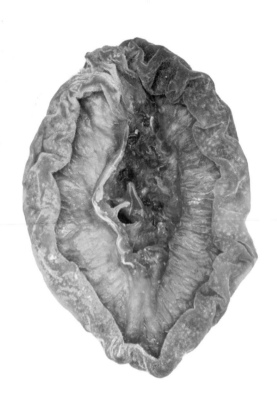

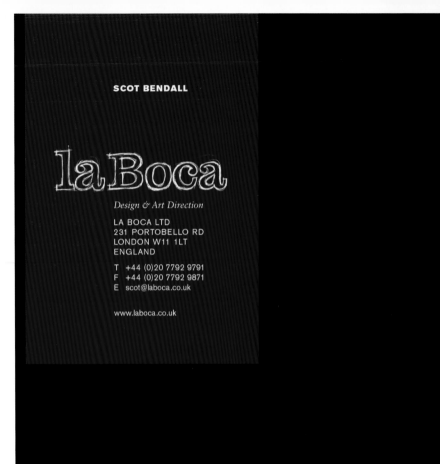

SCOT BENDALL

laBoca

Design & Art Direction

LA BOCA LTD
231 PORTOBELLO RD
LONDON W11 1LT
ENGLAND

T +44 (0)20 7792 9791
F +44 (0)20 7792 9871
E scot@laboca.co.uk

www.laboca.co.uk

Design/photography
Scot Bendall

For
La Boca_
Designer_
London, UK

Info
Having so often been asked the question "what is that?", Scot Bendall equates the success of a card with its ability to earn a double-take. The image of a dried fruit echoes the home page on La Boca's website which invites the viewer to "eat me". Rich colours and a sensual image reflect this design agency's work, producing printed matter for the film and music industries.

t: 56 84 73 62 / 04455 54 52 2649

hulahula.com.mx

quique@hulahula.com.mx

HULA+HULA

Cha! cha@hulahula.com.mx t: 56 84 73 62 / 04455 21 09 89 46 **hulahula**.com.mx

HULA · HULA

HULA · HULA

Quique Ottenwalder Uribe

Design
 Hula Hula

For
 Hula Hula_
 Designers_
 Bombass, Mexico

Info
 Tropical vegetation, an exuberant logo based on a continuous
 squiggle and rich, sunshine colours add up to maximum impact.

Design/photography
Ella Doran

For
Ella Doran Design_
Designer_
London, UK

Info
Ella puts her own and friends' photography on any number
of surfaces, from tableware to stationery; each year she adds
a new image to her gallery of business cards.

Ella Doran
Creative / Managing Director

Unit H, Ground Floor South
95 - 97 Redchurch Street,
London.
E2 7DJ

Tel: 020 7613 0782
Fax: 020 7613 0306

e-mail: ella@ella-doran.demon.co.uk
www: elladoran.co.uk

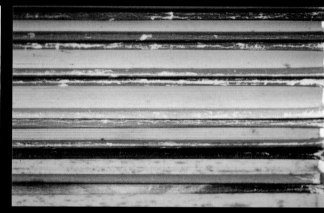

Mona Wiheden
Konsulent

Soda™ reklamebyrå
Dronningens gate 3
0152 Oslo
Mob 926 16 815
Tlf 22 33 29 13
Faks 22 42 94 85
www.sodareklame.no
mona.wiheden@sodareklame.no

Mona Wiheden
Konsulent

Soda™ reklamebyrå AS
Dronningens gate 3
0152 Oslo
Mob 926 16 815
Tlf 22 33 29 13
Faks 22 42 94 85
www.sodareklame.no
mona.wiheden@sodareklame.no

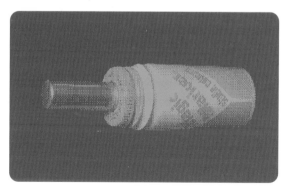

Design
Mission

For
Soda_
Advertising agency_
Oslo, Norway

Info
Rounded corners, funky colours and nostalgic half-tones; this set
of cards depicts vintage versions of tools of the trade – cameras,
televisions, computers and phones – hinting that this advertising
agency has a keen sense of humour.

Design
Big Block Creative

For
Kim Reed_
Stylist_
Melbourne,
Australia

Info
Echoing the format of collectable trading cards, the imagery for this stylist's card is culled from kitsch Japanese monster shows of the 1950s and '60s, a subject that excites much nerdish behaviour and fond recollections of a childhood spent in front of the TV.

Design
Big Block Creative

For
Nitrous Industries_
Designers_
Melbourne,
Australia

Info
Nitrous Industries is one of many incarnations of the designer
known to his friends as Woody, aka Big Block Creative. This
time he's indulging in nostalgia for a vintage age. By expertly
rendering a tactile facsimile of a crudely mechanical gaming
device, he shows off Nitrous Industries' significant imaging skills.

absolutezero°

	Address	Telephone
absolute zero degrees ltd	Unit 10 Empress Mews Kenbury Street London SE5 9BT	020 7737 6767

keith stephenson

m: 07989 109969
e: keith@absolutezerodegrees.com
w: www.absolutezerodegrees.com

<u>Design</u>
  Absolute Zero
  Degrees

<u>Photography</u>
  Ian Rippington

<u>For</u>
  Absolute Zero
  Degrees_
  Designers_
  London, UK

<u>Info</u>
A multi-disciplinary design consultancy, working for clients as
diverse as fashion brands and bands, their set of cards features
an interior design project; nostalgic, nature-inspired patterns
became wallpaper designs (working with Flo UK), printed using
traditional rollers and chalk-based inks.

Design/photography   For
Imke Oppenkamp   Imke Oppenkamp_
                                   Photographer_
                                   Liverpool, UK

Info
Rounded corners, family snapshots and "Blue Peter"
projects lend a personal, nostalgic air to this series
of cards for a young photographer.

verhuisd/moved Martijn Oostra————

studio, Donker Curtiusstraat 25e, NL-1051 JM Amsterdam—

tel/fax +31 (0)20 / 688 96 46——————————

e-mail studio@oostra.org——————————

Design/photography
Martijn Oostra

For
Martijn Oostra_
Designer_
Amsterdam,
The Netherlands

Info
This moving card features a classic El Camino pick-up
truck and the designer/photographer's new address.

Thorsten Geiger
GRAFIK DESIGN

CZARNIKAUER STR. 20A
10439 BERLIN

Telefon: 030 447 37 187
Telefax: 030 447 37 188

design@thorsten-geiger.de

Design/photography   For   Info
  Thorsten Geiger   Thorsten Geiger_   A graphic designer who creates his own photography, Thorsten
                        Designer_   Geiger has combined still-life, location, wildlife and archive
                        Berlin, Germany   shots in this series of cards, demonstrating his ability to compose
                                               images from disparate source materials.

James Sterling
Photography
M 07974 241 812

Design/photography
James Sterling

For
James Sterling_
Photographer_
London, UK

Info
Images of colour-saturated interior and exterior spaces
add up to a series of cards intended to demonstrate this
photographer's skills.

JIM FENWICK
PHOTOGRAPHER
LONDON
+44(0)7976292436
WWW.JIMFENWICK.COM
JIM@JIMFENWICK.COM

Design/photography
Jim Fenwick

For
Jim Fenwick_
Photographer_
London_ UK

Info
A series of staged images refer to birds, planes and flight –
concepts that are interpreted as broadly as possible.

> MATTHIAS FIEGL

> MANAGING DIRECTOR

> LOMOGRAPHIC SOCIETY INTERNATIONAL
> LOMOGRAPHISCHE AG, VIENNA
> HOLLERGASSE 41
> A-1150 VIENNA, AUSTRIA
> T +43-(0)1-899 44-0
> FIEGL@LOMOGRAPHY.COM

> WWW.LOMOGRAPHY.COM

Lomography
 Lomographic
 Society
 International

Design
 Bernard Winkler

For
 Lomographic
 Society
 International_
 Stock library_
 Worldwide

Info
The inexpensive Lomo camera from the former USSR sparked
an image-making revolution by encouraging people from around
the globe to look at their world in a new way. Housed at Lomo's
Vienna headquarters is a massive and varied archive of images
donated by Lomographers; this card series highlights the saturated
blues and reds unique to Lomo'd images.

<u>Design</u>
 Studio Elastik!

<u>Prints</u>
 Markus Schauer

<u>For</u>
 Nicole Gulotta_
 Fashion stylist_
 New York, USA

<u>Info</u>
 A cutting-edge fashion and editorial stylist, Nicole Gulotta
ensures the stylish images on her cards will never date by
featuring beautiful people from bygone eras, reprinted in
authentic tones from snap-shots found in vintage stores.

tel/fax: +1.212.744.5432
cell: +1.917.523.6289
hello@nicolegulotta.com
nicolegulotta.com

NICOLE · GULOTTA

christian petersen
photographer

www.flickr.com/photos/mysterycat/

mysterycatt@hotmail.com

<u>Design/photography</u>
Christian Petersen

<u>For</u>
Christian Petersen_
Photographer_
London, UK

<u>Info</u>
A self-initiated project, featuring women in a series of surreal locations, turns this photographer's business card into a mini-gallery.

VALERIE PHILLIPS
WEBBER REPRESENTS
393 BROADWAY
NEW YORK, NY
10013
212 343 7491

NEWYORK@WEBBERREPRESENTS.com

Photography
Valerie Phillips

For
Valerie Phillips_
Photographer_
New York, USA

Info
A fashion and editorial photographer, Valerie Phillips's cards
picture the individuals featured in her trilogy of books: an
investigation into the lives of three teenage girls growing
up in the USA.

Design
Alter

For
Alter_
Designers_
Melbourne,
Australia

Info
Created by a design duo that indulges in much hand-drawn
fun (including type and animation), these cards feature multiple
exposures of their creators jumping around, to dynamic effect.

www.viviancipolla.com
design@viviancipolla.com
luca de salvia
madelyn postman
1 hippodrome place
london w11 4ng
t +44 (0)20 7229 7878
f +44 (0)20 7229 6660

<u>Design/photography</u>
Madelyn Postman
Luca de Salvia

<u>For</u>
Vivian Cipolla_
Designers_
London, UK

<u>Info</u>
Creating a fictional character to represent their design
company, which works with high-end luxury and fashion
brands, this design duo dreamt up scenarios bearing Vivian's
name: under her doorbell, contact details are written on a
scrap of paper and the details of a meeting appear on a
stranger's hand.

NOWWASHYOURHANDS
UNITEDKINGDOM
DESIGNCOMPANY

Alex Amelines
Senior Animator
alex@nowwashyourhands.com

NOWWASHYOURHANDS
2ND FLOOR
48 POLAND STREET
LONDON
W1F 7ND

T: 020 7851 7080
F: 020 7851 7090

www.nowwashyourhands.com

NOWWASHYOURHANDS
UNITEDKINGDOM
DESIGNCOMPANY

Alison Jordan
Project Manager
alison@nowwashyourhands.com

NOWWASHYOURHANDS
2ND FLOOR
48 POLAND STREET
LONDON
W1F 7ND

T: 020 7851 7080
F: 020 7851 7090

www.nowwashyourhands.com

NOWWASHYOURHANDS
UNITEDKINGDOM
DESIGNCOMPANY

Angus Mackinnon
Creative Director
gus@nowwashyourhands.com

NOWWASHYOURHANDS
2ND FLOOR
48 POLAND STREET
LONDON
W1F 7ND

M: 07767 703661
T: 020 7851 7080
F: 020 7851 7090

www.nowwashyourhands.com

Design
  NOWWASHYOURHANDS

Photography
  Chris Hewitt

For
  NOWWASHYOURHANDS_
  Designers_
  London, UK

Info
  The boardroom table was carpeted with turf and each
  staff member was photographed lying on top of it, eyes
  open and closed; proof that a simple idea may produce
  the oddest results.

NOWWASHYOURHANDS
UNITEDKINGDOM
DESIGNCOMPANY

Bob Silver
Design Director
bob@nowwashyourhands.com

NOWWASHYOURHANDS
2ND FLOOR
48 POLAND STREET
LONDON
W1F 7ND

M: 07939 627837
T: 020 7851 7080
F: 020 7851 7090

www.nowwashyourhands.com

NOWWASHYOURHANDS
UNITEDKINGDOM
DESIGNCOMPANY

Laure Baudon
laure@nowwashyourhands.com

NOWWASHYOURHANDS
2ND FLOOR
48 POLAND STREET
LONDON
W1F 7ND

T: 020 7851 7080
F: 020 7851 7090

www.nowwashyourhands.com

NOWWASHYOURHANDS
UNITEDKINGDOM
DESIGNCOMPANY

Neil Jeffries
Managing Director
neil@nowwashyourhands.com

NOWWASHYOURHANDS
2ND FLOOR
48 POLAND STREET
LONDON
W1F 7ND

M: 07904 517248
T: 020 7851 7080
F: 020 7851 7090

www.nowwashyourhands.com

NOWWASHYOURHANDS
UNITEDKINGDOM
DESIGNCOMPANY

Anna Lindequist
Project Manager
anna@nowwashyourhands.com

NOWWASHYOURHANDS
2ND FLOOR
48 POLAND STREET
LONDON
W1F 7ND

T: 020 7851 7080
F: 020 7851 7090

www.nowwashyourhands.com

NOWWASHYOURHANDS
UNITEDKINGDOM
DESIGNCOMPANY

Kevin Coffey
Designer
kevin@nowwashyourhands.com

NOWWASHYOURHANDS
2ND FLOOR
48 POLAND STREET
LONDON
W1F 7ND

T: 020 7851 7080
F: 020 7851 7090

www.nowwashyourhands.com

NOWWASHYOURHANDS
UNITEDKINGDOM
DESIGNCOMPANY

Lisa Mesztig
Account Director
lisa@nowwashyourhands.com

NOWWASHYOURHANDS
2ND FLOOR
48 POLAND STREET
LONDON
W1F 7ND

M: 07786 515786
T: 020 7851 7080
F: 020 7851 7090

www.nowwashyourhands.com

**NOWWASHYOURHANDS
UNITEDKINGDOM
DESIGNCOMPANY**

Robin Evans
Flash Developer
robin@nowwashyourhands.com

NOWWASHYOURHANDS
2ND FLOOR
48 POLAND STREET
LONDON
W1F 7ND

T: 020 7851 7080
F: 020 7851 7090

www.nowwashyourhands.com

**NOWWASHYOURHANDS
UNITEDKINGDOM
DESIGNCOMPANY**

Jamie Warren
Senior Developer
jamie@nowwashyourhands.com

NOWWASHYOURHANDS
2ND FLOOR
48 POLAND STREET
LONDON
W1F 7ND

T: 020 7851 7080
F: 020 7851 7090

www.nowwashyourhands.com

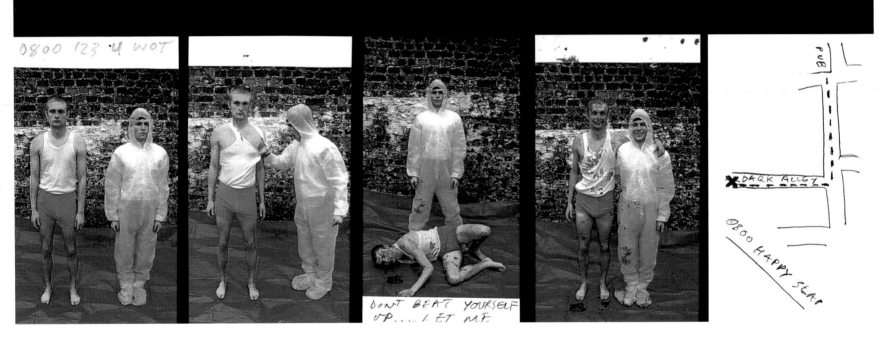

Design
 Orlando Weeks

For
 Orlando Weeks_
 Image-maker/
 musician_
 Brighton, UK

Info
Solving the problem of designing a card for someone with
multiple careers, Orlando Weeks's tongue-in-cheek approach
was to depict a "fix-it" scenario. On a practical level, this
distinctive card won't be missed; and while it is devoid of
contact details, patches of blank space mean specially
tailored data may be added by hand.

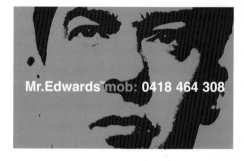

Design
Neil Edwards

For
Mr. Edwards_
Designer_
Sydney, Australia

Info
Letting you know he means business, Mr. Edwards's alternative
card presents an in-your-face, close-cropped portrait of a
Mr. Kray, one of the legendary criminal twins from London's
Swinging Sixties.

Design/photography
Enterprise IG

For
Enterprise IG_
Designers_
London, UK

Info
A comprehensive series of "found type" initials represents this
global brand agency; a simple idea but infinitely variable.

ENTERPRISE IG

THE GLOBAL BRAND AGENCY

Robin Kadrnka
Group Marketing Director

robin.kadrnka@enterpriseig.com

D +44 (0)20 7559 7073   11-33 St. John Street,
T +44 (0)20 7559 7000   London EC1M 4PJ,
F +44 (0)20 7559 7001   United Kingdom
M +44 (0)7970 842 103   www.enterpriseig.com

Design
Oliver

For
Oliver_
Designer_
London, UK

Info
Infinite variation is achieved by overprinting onto
an appropriated ready-made – paint swatches
from a local DIY store.

219

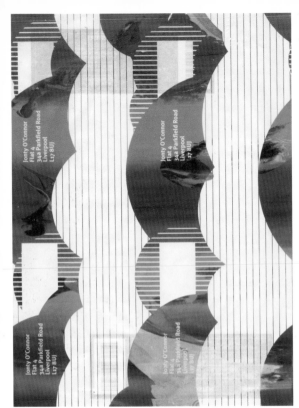
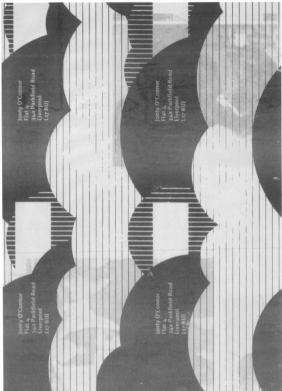
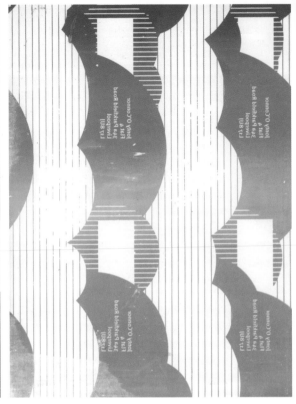

Design/photography
Jonty O'Connor

For
Jonty O'Connor_
Designer_
Liverpool, UK

Info
Hoarding "useless" printouts, including proofs, emails and
mistakes, and then screen-printing onto the reverse using
left-over ink (hence the marbling), Jonty O'Connor converts
scraps into a set of unique business cards.

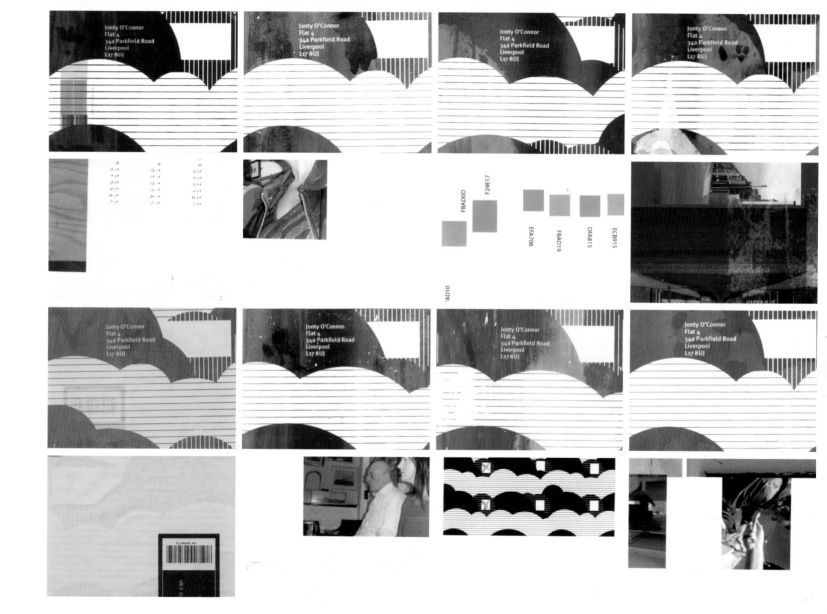

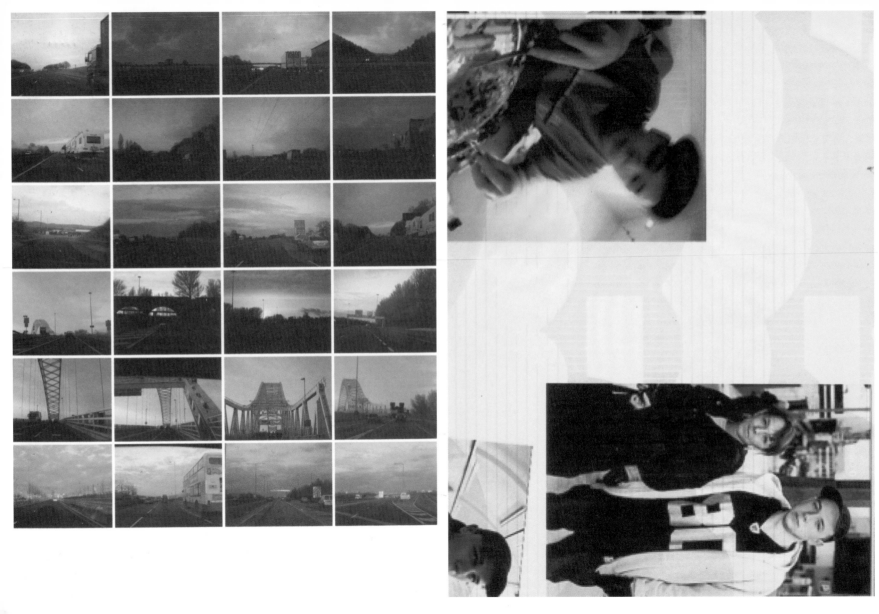

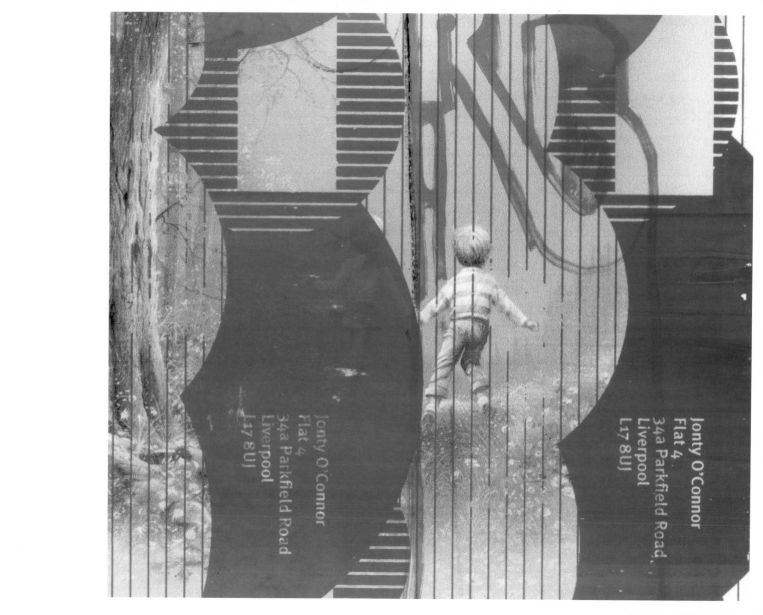

Jonty O'Connor
Flat 4,
34a Parkfield Road
Liverpool
L17 8UJ

Jonty O'Connor
Flat 4,
34a Parkfield Road
Liverpool
L17 8UJ

Jonty O'Connor
Flat 4,
34a Parkfield Road
Liverpool
L17 8UJ

we print in-house onto lots of different substrates

Design/illustration
mws

For
mws_
Designers_
London_ UK

Info
Versatile image-makers and muralists mws carry their DIY, "can-do" attitude over onto their business cards; they're as confident using fabric and sewing machines as they are with stencils, spray-paint, appropriated imagery and all forms of card and paper stock.

do call!

t/f. 0207 720 2100

e : matt.wingfield@virgin.net

we draw, paint & spray imagery direct to walls & windows

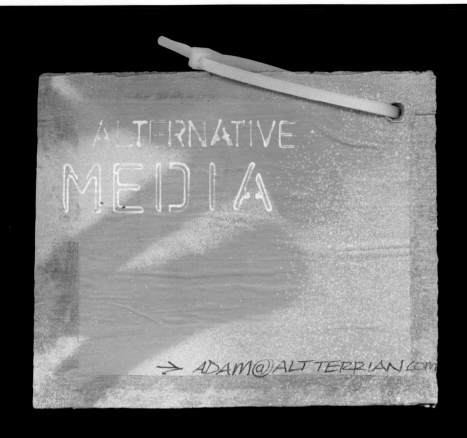

Design/illustration
Wombat

For
ALT-TERRAIN_
Marketing_
Boston, USA

Info
Hand-made cards of various sizes, materials and media
produced by a posse of street and graffiti artists working
for a guerrilla marketing company. Spray-paint, marker pen,
cardboard and faux-packaging echo the graphic language
of the street.

→ alt·Terrain

20% more

www.ALTTERRAIN.com — 617·442·8357 —

FRESH CUSTOMIZ MEDI

• ALT·TERRAIN

1127 HARRISON AVE.
BOSTON MA.   02119

CUSTOMIZED MARKETING

www.ALTTERRAIN.com

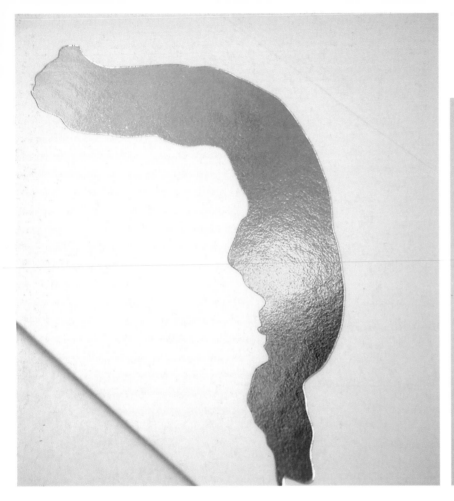

Design
Jen Wu

For
Temporary
Contemporary_
Art space/gallery_
London, UK

Info
Designed while on a residency in Shanghai, where the low cost of printing enabled
Jen Wu to indulge herself and use gold, which in China is emblematic of success.
Throwing the onus of understanding back onto the viewer, the design includes a
deliberately vague shape – is it the island of Taiwan, a woman's profile or "solid-
gold faeces"? This ambiguity echoes the wide-open possibilities of Temporary
Contemporary, a short-term, artist-run gallery located in a redevelopment site.

ORG inc.
315 W 39th St
Studio 911
NY, NY 10018
212 563 5900
http://www.o-r-g.com/

Design
  David Reinfurt

For
  ORG inc_
  Designer_
  New York, USA

Info
  This deceptively simple design is in fact the result of real-time
  monitoring of the New York Commodities Market; the amount
  of gold foil and the thickness of each letter relate to fluctuations
  in the price of gold on the morning the card was designed.

Dan Moscrop
Managing Director
Them Design Limited
The Holywell Centre
1 Phipp Street
London EC2A 4PS
+44(0)207 613 0080
+44(0)7989 599 767
dan@them.co.uk
www.them.co.uk

Adrian Britteon
Creative Director
Them Design Limited
The Holywell Centre
1 Phipp Street
London EC2A 4PS
+44(0)207 613 0080
+44(0)7868 746 941
ade@them.co.uk
www.them.co.uk

Adrian Wong
Senior Web Designer
Them Design Limited
The Holywell Centre
1 Phipp Street
London EC2A 4PS
+44(0)207 613 0080
+44(0)7978 544 626
adrian@them.co.uk
www.them.co.uk

Charlie Dawson
New Business Director
Them Design Limited
The Holywell Centre
1 Phipp Street
London EC2A 4PS
+44(0)207 613 0080
+44(0)7786 023 991
charlie@them.co.uk
www.them.co.uk

Design
Them

For
Them_
Designers_
London, UK

Info
Using Perspex to great effect, this design group employs the most basic language of print, the dot matrix, to create a brand. Overlaying and twisting various blocks of printed dots produces myriad patterns, from mechanistic hexagons to organic flowers. The final images are printed onto Perspex cards.

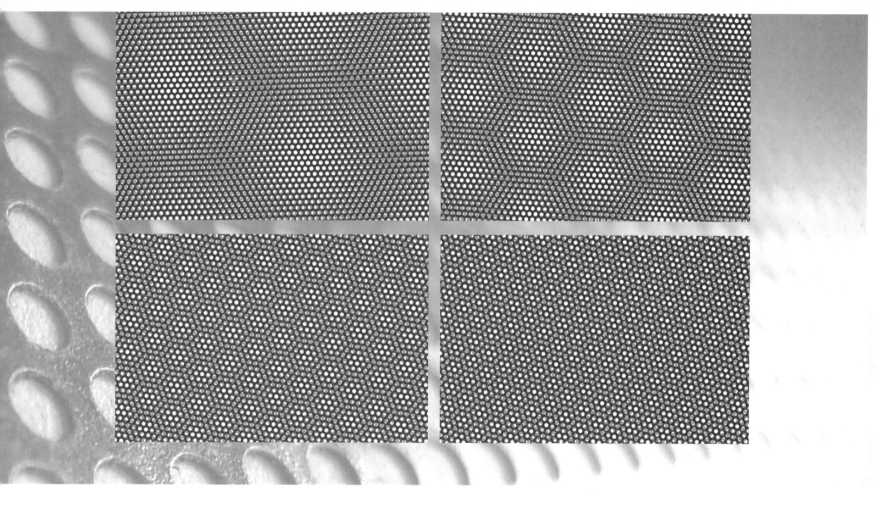

never trust a stylist*

*William Baker : Creative Director Tel/Fax 020 7813 1913
7 Caple Street, London, WC1A 1HX Email Alex.bc2000@aol.com

never trust a stylist*

*William Baker - Creative Director Tel/Fax 020 7813 1913
Street, London, WC1A 1NH Email Alexdex2000@aol.com

Design
Tony Hung

For
William Baker_
Stylist_
London, UK

Info
Stylist to the stars William Baker's tongue-in-cheek(y) message
is silkscreened onto neon-edged acrylic for maximum, glow-in-
the-dark effect. Tony Hung hit on the idea of neon when he
learnt that William conducts his business in the neon-lit arena
that is London's Soho.

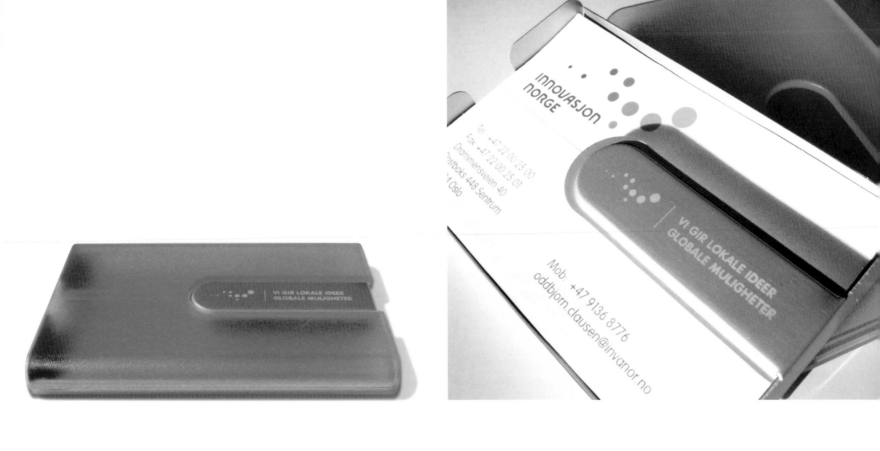

INNOVASJON NORGE

Tel: +47 22 00 25 00
Fax: +47 22 42 96 11
Akersgata 13
Postboks 448 Sentrum
0158 Oslo, Norway

ASTRID MARIE THIIS EVENSEN
Stillingsnavn
Stillingsnavn

Dir tel: +47 2200 2701
Mob: +47 9575 8534
astrid-mari.this-evensen@invanor.no

VI GIR LOKALE IDEER GLOBALE MULIGHETER
www.invanor.no

Design
  Mission

For
  Innovasjon Norge_
  Development
  agency_
  Oslo, Norway

Info
  A futuristic card solution for Norway's state-run development
  company incorporates a distinctive green plastic cover and
  silver holder; the cards remain pristine and are easily dispensed.

artless mind

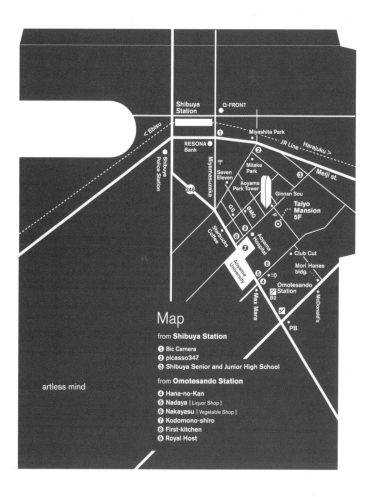

Design
Artless

For
Artless_
Designers_
Tokyo, Japan

Info
Multi-tasking designers, as happy instigating their own cultural projects as they are working across all media, Artless's card is as much an artefact as it is a communication device, incorporating a map (essential in Tokyo), a durable faux-credit card and a colour-coded holder.

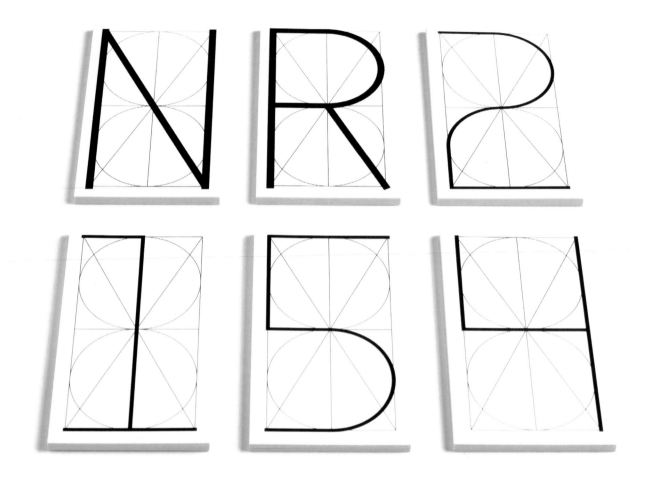

Design
 Troels Faber_
 Jacob Wildschiødtz

For
 NR2154_
 Designers_
 Copenhagen,
 Denmark

Info
 On one side of these cards is printed a typographic grid and
 the various elements of this design duo's identity; on the reverse
 each partner rubber-stamps their contact details.

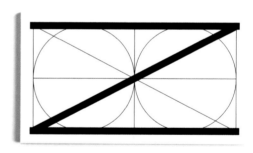

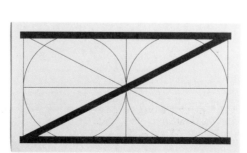

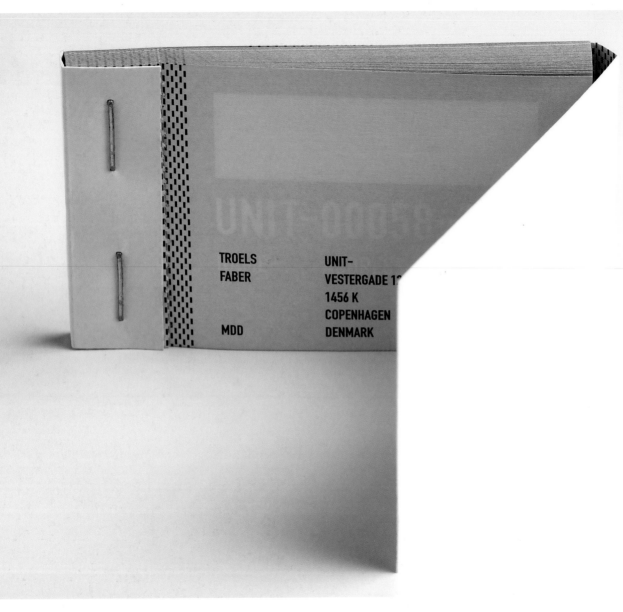

Design
Troels Faber_
Jacob Wildschiødtz_
Henrik Norberg_
Satoru Inoue

For
Unit-1391_
Designers_
Copenhagen,
Denmark

Info
A sophisticated but visually understated solution to carrying
a stack of business cards, this individualized notepad is housed
in a "matchbook" cover and perforated for ease of use.

Design/illustration
Maki

For
Maki_
Illustrators_
Groningen,
The Netherlands

Info
Every business card from these designers is an invitation to "filter" some ideas over a coffee; they are created using the office's inkjet printer and real filters. They also double as little gift bags.

Design
Paula Benson_
Nick Hard_
Claire Warner_
Paul West_
Form

For
Granite_
Printers_
Essex, UK

Info
Demonstrating the potential of an elegant two-tone stock,
Form underline the solidity of this company's name logotype;
debossed and varnished, it is both tactile and robust.

Piccalilikus

Design/illustration
Jon Burgerman

For
Jon Burgerman_
Illustrator_
Nottingham, UK

Info
With a kid's printing set, illustrator Jon Burgerman adds essential contact details to corrugated-cardboard backings on his very own character-based stickers. Roughly cut out by hand, each card is a unique mini-artwork.

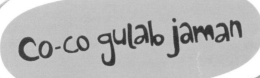

Co-co gulab jaman

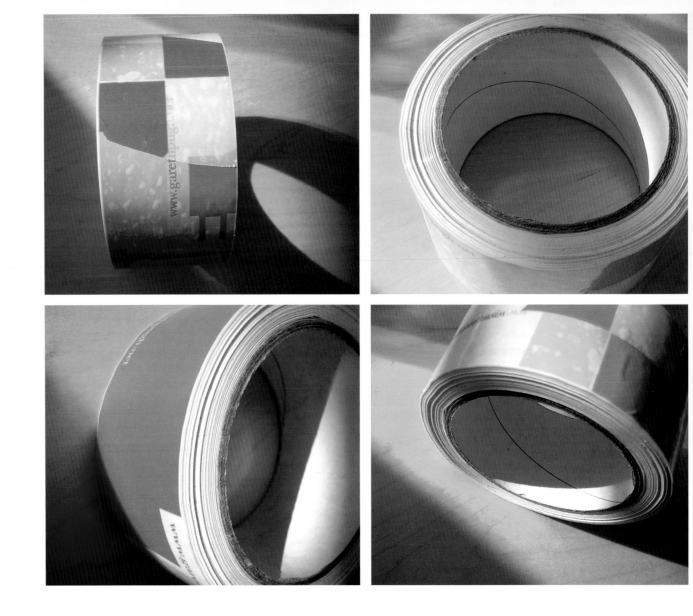

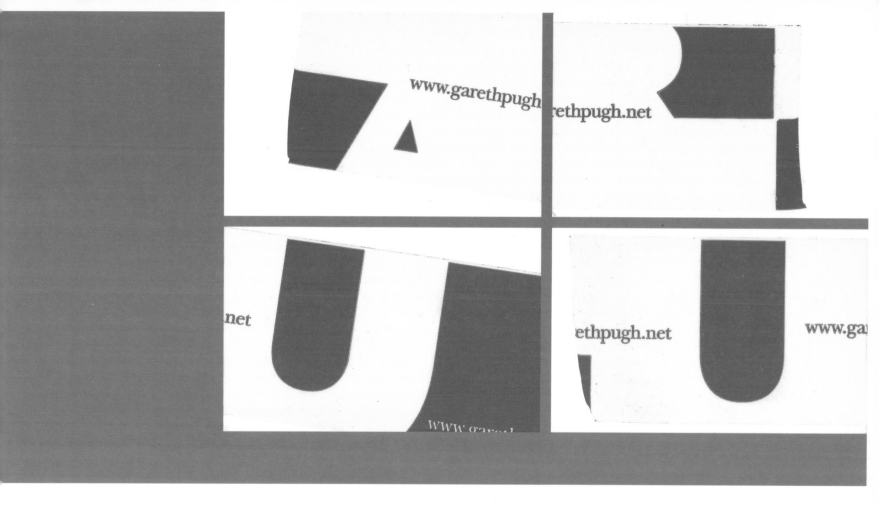

Design
  Jenny & Byron

For
  Gareth Pugh_
  Fashion designer_
  London, UK

Info
  Unique, hand-made, affordable cards may be produced quickly
  and whenever necessary, using personalized packing tape;
  simply cut any stock to size and get sticking.

Design
TAK!

For
TAK!_
Designers_
Birmingham, UK

Info
A design group working across disciplines from illustration
to games development, Tak! have been involved in the
now-ubiquitous sticker revolution; their card comes with
a self-promotional button badge.

Design
Hugh Frost

For
Hugh Frost_
Designer_
Brighton, UK

Info
Hugh Frost (of design collective Posikids, publishers of Math magazine) offers several display options with his card: a fridge magnet, paperclip and noticeboard pin are neatly packaged in a zip-lock baggie.

249

ANDREWTILLER
TILLERWILLIAMS.
COM

Design
TillerWilliams

For
TillerWilliams_
Designers_
London, UK

Info
Using "stencil" type to best effect, this die-cut card
is understated and restrained, but oozes attitude.

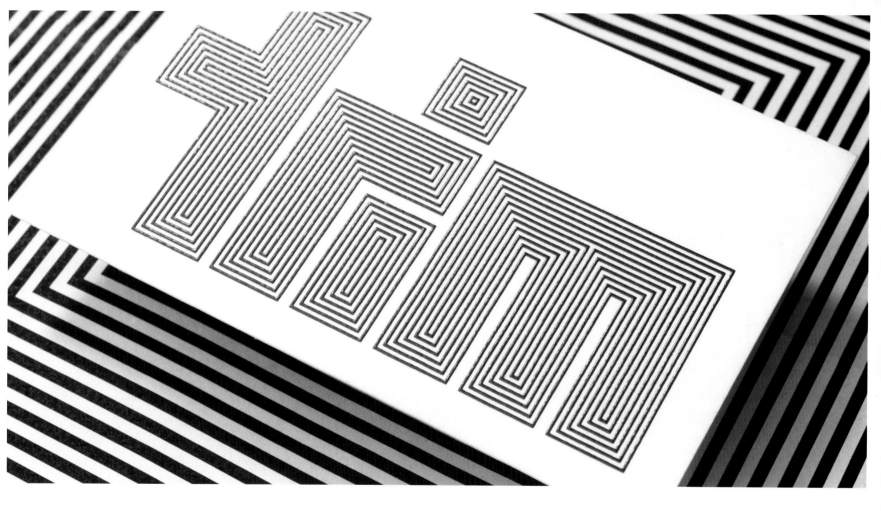

Design
 Multistorey

For
 Trim_
 Film & video editors_
 London, UK

Info
For a film- and video-editing house, an interlocking, linear
logotype reminiscent of optical illusions (caused, perhaps,
by staring too long at a screen) was further enhanced using
thermographic printing. The resultant tactile, raised surface
intensifies the three-dimensional quality.

1. Background

2. Figure

3. Result >>>

* Belio-logo (stencil version)
Instructions: Cut and paint

BELIO MAGAZINE

Calle Argente 14.
28053 Madrid. Spain.
Tlf/Fax: (0034) 91 478 25 26
e-mail: info@beliomagazine.com
http://www.beliomagazine.com

Design
Gee.Oh.Dee

For
Belio Magazine_
Online and print
magazine_
Madrid, Spain

Info
The card for this street-art magazine gives lessons in how
to stencil, and a mini-design ready to cut out and spray.

Gee.Oh.Dee
Pablo & Javier IA: Art, Design, Edition, Events production, Dj...

BE 10 | K4 05 | drum'n' NOISE

01 Javier IA (Call me: 626 225 770)
C/ Argente 14. 28053 Madrid. Spain
javier@beliomagazine.com
www.geeohdee.com

1577 5070

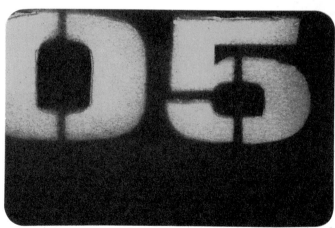

Gee.Oh.Dee
Pablo & Javier IA: Art, Design, Edition, Events production, Dj...

BE 10 | K4 05 | drum'n' NOISE

02 Pablo IA (Call me: 636 163 955)
C/ Argente 14. 28053 Madrid. Spain
pablo@beliomagazine.com
www.geeohdee.com

1577 5070

Design
Gee.Oh.Dee

For
Gee.Oh.Dee_
Designers/DJs/
editors_
Madrid, Spain

Info
The design department of street-art magazine Belio are also DJs,
a record label and events organizers; their cards sport a number
of logos, with a colour-coded version for each partner.

Design
Simon Slater

For
Laki 139_
Designer_
West Sussex, UK

Info
Simon is unique among designers in that he prefers to make
one-off objects. His cards reflect his hand-marked, distressed
aesthetic as each sports a different logo and has been sprayed
with a thin solution of bleach, turning the board a luminous gold.

Design/illustration
Spencer Wilson

For
Spencer Wilson_
Illustrator_
London, UK

Info
Street-inspired artist and illustrator Spencer spray-paints onto
board, screenprints his card design and then trims it to size,
guaranteeing that each one is unique.

NOGGINS+

A SLICE ᵒᶠ JAPAN

MARK'S LITTLE Book ABoUT KINDER EGGS...

OPEN   CLOSED

↓ DISINFOTAINMENT ↓

P.O.Box 664 London E3 4QR

STAY FREE

HNSHAW

JUXTAPOZ

↑ MARK PAWSON ↑
www.mpawson.demon.co.uk

machina mundana

Equilicua

BLINKY

Jeffrey Vallance

So' BOY

MINI FIGURINE

13 Books

Copyright Violation Squad

I ♥

RAT FINK

DF

Design
Mark Pawson

For
Mark Pawson_
Designer_
London, UK

Info
A prodigious creator of image-based products and distributor
of other artists' work, Mark Pawson uses his business card as
a mini-catalogue. He's hand-printed over 2,000 cards in various
colourways using the idiosyncratic Print Gocco device. Look
closely and you'll see new products appear as others sell out;
collect the set.

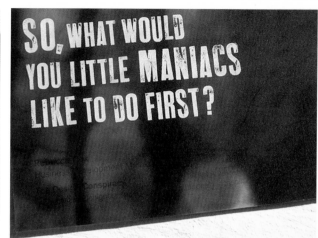

Design
Christiaan Vermaas_
OFFICE OF CC

For
OFFICE OF CC_
Designer_
Amsterdam,
The Netherlands

Info
The instant aesthetic of burning a brand into wood, denoting heat and passion, is used to create a series of cards; choose the most appropriate for a meeting, whether it declares an outspoken muttering, a personal proclamation or simply an email address.

FRANCESCA
WADE

www.posikids.org
+44 [0]7980 754545

FRANCESCA
WADE

www.posikids.org
+44 [0]7980 754545

FRANCESCA
WADE

www.posikids.org
+44 [0]7980 754545

Design
 Francesca Wade

For
 Francesca Wade_
 Artist_
 Brighton, UK

Info
 Francesca Wade is as happy creating clothing as she is
 designing and editing Math magazine, just one of the projects
 instigated by Posikids (the design collective she's a member of).
 Each card is hand-stitched to ensure maximum individuality.

Design
Mark Wood

For
Mark Wood_
Designer_
London, UK

Mark Wood's expertise is in branding and he needed a
memorable card: "my name + branding = a wooden business
card". Using a brass die, heated over a gas hob, Mark imprints
swatches of wood veneer cut to size.

<u>Design</u>
 Sweaty Betty

<u>For</u>
 Mini Mart_
 Cool shop_
 Brighton, UK

<u>Info</u>
 Combining the vernacular, star-shaped fluorescent cards of
 discount shops worldwide with a custom-made rubber stamp,
 each Mini Mart card is a one-off; bags and price tags reinforce
 the aesthetic.

Design
  Kate Moross

For
  Think Prolific_
  Designer_
  London, UK

Info
A specially made rubber-stamp and a DIY stamp kit provide an infinitely flexible identity for a unique networking portal. Via a website set up by Kate to raise the profile of young talent, from hairdressers to painters and tattoo artists, she reps her gang of creative types online. Hard-copy communications are produced using paper and card flotsam and jetsam, thus promoting recycling.

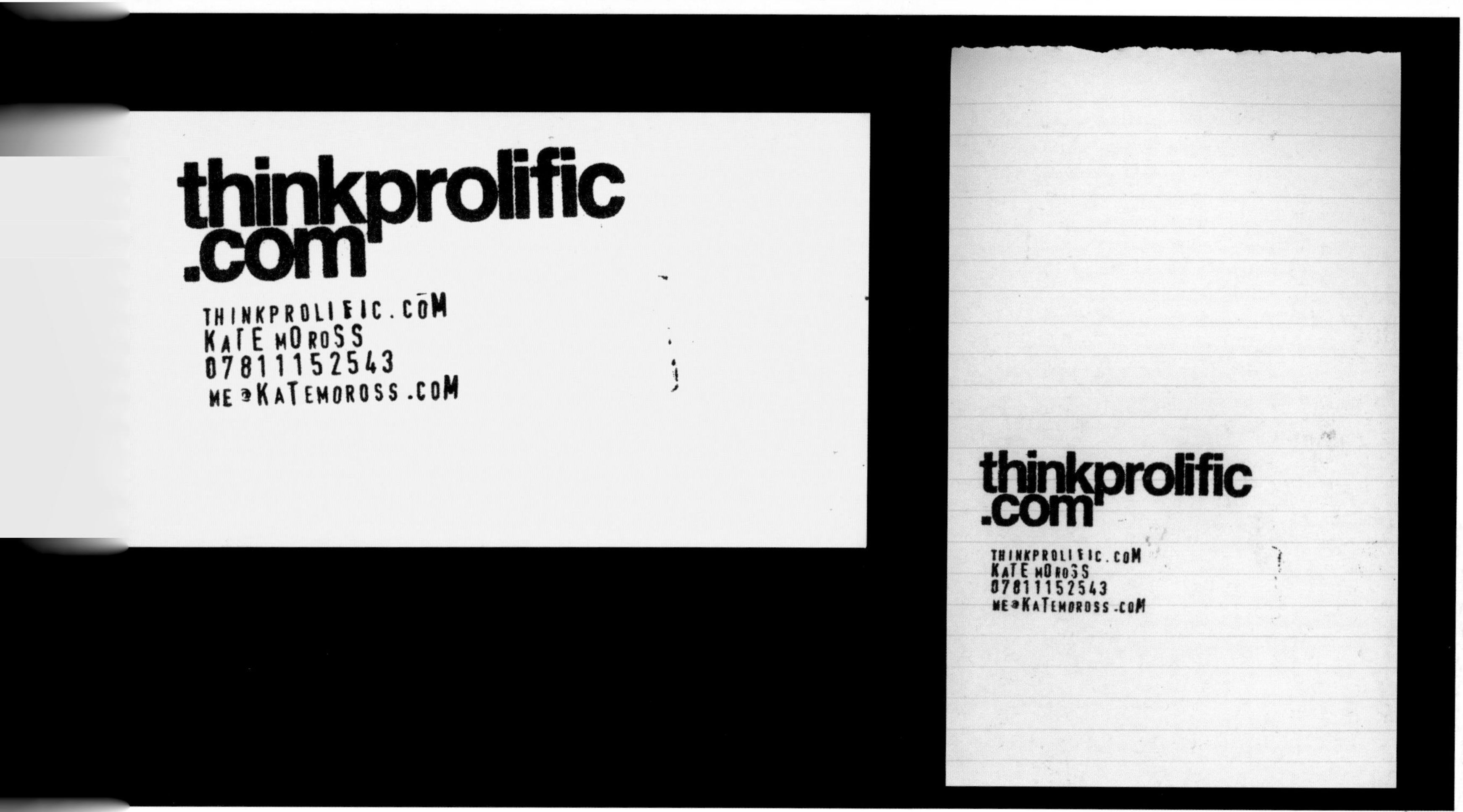

thinkprolific
.com

THINKPROLIFIC.COM
KATE MOROSS
07811152543
ME@KATEMOROSS.COM

thinkprolific
.com

THINKPROLIFIC.COM
KATE MOROSS
07811152543
ME@KATEMOROSS.COM

Design
Zookeeper

For
Galet Shop_
Pebble shop_
Tabis, France

Info
Hand-painted pebbles are the only way to advertise
a shop that sells the same.

Design
Tofer

For
Tofer_
Artist_
Los Angeles, USA

Info
A guerrilla-style artist, as at home in a gallery as he is postering the streets of LA, Tofer adopts the ubiquitous matchbook as a vehicle for getting his name and logo out there. Placed on tables in a bar or handed to a stranger, they're highly likely to be pocketed.